GEORGE BELL AND
NIKOLAI VELIMIROVIĆ

The Story of a Friendship

Dr Muriel Heppell

GEORGE BELL
AND
NIKOLAI VELIMIROVIĆ

The Story of a Friendship

LAZARICA PRESS
BIRMINGHAM
2001

ISBN 0 948298 18 9

Published and Printed in Great Britain by
LAZARICA PRESS
Serbian Orthodox Church of the Holy Prince Lazar
131 Cob Lane, Birmingham B30 1QE, England

To

Alicia Cortés de Allen

in gratitude for our friendship

CONTENTS

ILLUSTRATIONS

PREFACE

The form of this short study evolved gradually, over a considerable period of time. When I first had the idea of writing the story of the friendship between the two principal characters portrayed here, I felt that it was important that it should be told, as far as possible, in their own words and the words of those who knew them. My main source was the correspondence of the two bishops, preserved in the papers of Bishop George Bell in Lambeth Palace Library; I also used the papers of Canon J. A. Douglas. This task was made both easy and pleasant, thanks to the help of Melanie Barber, deputy librarian and archivist at Lambeth Palace Library, to whom I owe a special debt of gratitude. For much of the background reading, I used books borrowed from Dr Williams's Library, and I would like to thank the trustees and staff of that library for their help. I should also like to express my special thanks to Archbishop Rowan Williams for writing the Foreword, and to James Chrismas for making the drawing of Chichester Cathedral, which Bishop Nikolai visited during his short stay in England after the Second World War.

A number of people have read the manuscript, and offered both helpful suggestions and encouragement: George Novaković, who provided background information about Bishop Nikolai's life in the inter-war period, not easily available to me elsewhere; Dr Rebecca Beaconsfield, the Revd Dr Colin Davey and the Revd Kevin Morris. To all of them I extend my sincere thanks.

Muriel Heppell

iii

FOREWORD

This book is a long-overdue introduction to a profoundly important moment in the ecumenical history of the twentieth century. The recent tragic history of what had been Yugoslavia has further overlaid what was already an almost-forgotten aspect of relations between Britain and Serbia, the period in the last days of the First World War and afterwards when the still-struggling Serbian nation looked to Britain and to the Church of England for aid in reconstructing their common life and renewing their Church - and were not wholly disappointed.

Bishop Nikolai Velimirović was, for several generations of British Anglicans, one of that group of unmistakeable moral and spiritual giants who brought something of the depth and challenge of the Orthodox world into the West. It was in these post-war years that he first made the contacts that were to touch the lives of so many; and especially the contact with an Anglican giant of the spirit, George Bell. Too few of Bell's admirers know of this friendship and may be surprised to find him so sympathetically involved in the Orthodox world. But it is an inspiration to read not only of co-operation between the two but of the mutual learning and stimulation that their friendship brought. In their shared and passionate resistance to totalitarianism and their obstinate concern for its victims, they drew on the same wells of theological vision, on the heritage common to Anglicans and Orthodox of an early-Christian theology and spirituality in which the pervasive sense of God's glory, God's image, in the heart of God's human creatures made it impossible to ignore or forget the sufferings of those the world would happily overlook.

Perhaps reconciliation and understanding between Churches happens most profoundly when that vision is recovered, shared and acted upon together. I hope that this excellent study will help to renew just such a sharing. I know too that it will help to lessen the astonishing ignorance in this country about the real history of Serbia and its neighbours, and about the rôle of the Orthodox Church, not as an uncritical champion of narrow nationalism in the region but, at its best, a vital voice in the creation of a society ready to take its full part in a new Europe. Bishop Nikolai's life and witness could hardly be bettered as an illustration of how this rôle could be worked out, and we owe a real debt to Dr Heppell for her labours in bringing again to light this considerable figure in the story of modern European Christianity, and allowing us to overhear his searching and moving conversation with Bishop Bell, for so many people the voice of Anglican integrity at its clearest. Anglicans and Orthodox alike will learn from this fresh and authoritative work.

+Rowan Williams
Archbishop of Wales

COPYRIGHT ACKNOWLEDGMENTS

Passages from the letters and papers of Bishop George Bell, Archbishop Randall Davidson and Canon J. A. Douglas have been used by kind permission of Lambeth Palace Library.

Passages from R. C. D. Jasper, *George Bell: Bishop of Chichester* (OUP, 1967) are reproduced by permission of Dr David Jasper.

Passages from G. K. A. Bell, *Randall Davidson, Archbishop of Canterbury* (2nd Edition, OUP, 1938) are quoted by permission of the Oxford University Press.

Passages from Hugh and Christopher Seton-Watson, *The Making of a New Europe* (Methuen, 1981), are reproduced by permission of Routledge.

Passages from *Black Lamb and Grey Falcon* by Rebecca West (Copyright Rebecca West, 1940), are reprinted by permission of PFD on behalf of the estate of Dame Rebecca.

A passage (93 words) from *The Kingship of Christ* by G. K. A. Bell, Bishop of Chichester (Penguin Books, 1954), is reproduced by permission of Penguin Books Ltd.

The drawing of Chichester Cathedral is reproduced with the permission of the artist, James Chrismas.

BIBLIOGRAPHY

Unpublished material:

> George Bell Papers, Vols. 190, 200, 79, 354, 247, 258.
> Randall Davidson Papers, Vol. 520 (# 70-109).
> Douglas Papers, Vol. 51.

Published works:

> Alexander, Stella, *The Triple Myth: A Life of Archbishop Alojzije Stepinac,* East European Monographs CCXXVI, Boulder, 1987.

> Bell, G. K. A., *Randall Davidson, Archbishop of Canterbury,* 2nd Edition, Oxford University Press, 1938.

> Bell, G. K. A., *The Kingship of Christ,* Penguin Special, 1954.

> Benz, E., *The Eastern Orthodox Church,* New York, 1963.

> Chadwick, Owen, *Michael Ramsey. A Life,* Oxford University Press, 1991.

> Chandler, Michael, *The Life and Work of John Mason Neale,* London, Gracewing, 1995.

> Cokić, Dragoljub, *Vladika Nikolai - moja razmišljanja i sećanja* (Bishop Nikolai - my reflections and memories), Ridgefield, New Jersey, 1996 (contains interesting insights into Bishop Nikolai's later years in America).

> Dobrijević, Irinej Mirko, *Bishop Nicholai Velimirović: a Contemporary Orthodox Witness,* Serbian Studies Vol. 10, 1996, pp. 198-209.

Durham, Thomas, *Serbia: the Rise and Fall of a Medieval Empire,* Ebor Press, York, 1989.

Emmert, Thomas A., *Serbian Golgotha: Kosovo, 1389,* East European Monographs, CCLXXVIII, New York, 1990.

Field, Frank, *George Bell: A Uniquely Consistent Life,* Lambeth Palace Library Annual Review, 1996, pp. 51-62.

Godjević-Subotić, Anna, *Povodom desetogodišnice smrti Vladike Nikolaja* (On the occasion of the tenth anniversary of the death of Bishop Nikolai), *Glasnik srpskog istorisko-kulturnog društva 'Njegoš'* (Journal of the Serbian Historical and Cultural Society 'Njegoš'), December, 1966, pp. 94-101.

Heppell, Muriel, *The Ecclesiastical Career of Gregory Camblak,* London, 1979.

Heppell, M. and Singleton, F. B., *Yugoslavia,* Ernest Benn (Nations of the Modern World Series), London, 1961.

Jasper, R. C. D., *George Bell, Bishop of Chichester,* Oxford University Press, 1967.

Langdon, John W., *July 1914: The Long Debate, 1918-1990,* New York and Oxford, 1991.

Leech, Kenneth, *Soul Friend,* 1961.

Lees, Michael, *The Rape of Serbia,* London & New York, 1990.

Lough, A. G., *The Influence of John Mason Neale,* London, SPCK, 1962.

Mihailović, Vasa, ed., *Landmarks in Serbian Culture and History,* Serb National Federation, Pittsburg, 1983.

Moss, C. B., *The Old Catholic Movement: its Origins and History,* London, SPCK, 1948.

Purcell, William, *Fisher of Lambeth: A Portrait from Life,* London, Hodder and Stoughton, 1969.

Robertson, Edwin, *Unshakeable Friend. George Bell and the German Churches,* London, CCBI, 1995.

Seton-Watson, Hugh and Seton-Watson, Christoper, *The Making of a New Europe,* London, Methuen, 1981.

Slijepčević, Đoko, *Istorija Srpske pravoslavne crkve* (History of the Serbian Orthodox Church), Vol. III, Cologne, 1986.

Temperley, H. V. A., *A History of Serbia,* London, 1919.

Velimirović, Nikolai, *Serbia's Place in Human History,* London, 1915.

Velimirović, Nikolai, *Religion and Nationality in Serbia* (translated by Fanny Copeland), London, 1915.

Velimirović, Nikolai, *Serbia in Light and Darkness,* London, 1916.

Velimirović, Nikolai, *The Lord's Prayer: a Devout Interpretation,* London, 1916.

Velimirović, Nikolai, *Sermons on Subjects Suggested by the War,* London, 1916.

Velimirović, Nikolai, *The Children of the Illuminator,* London, 1919.

Velimirović, Nikolai, *The Spiritual Rebirth of Europe,* London, Faith Press, 1920.

Velimirović, Nikolai, *The Life of St Sava,* New York, 1952.

Velimirović, Nikolai, *Prayers by the Lake,* translated and annotated by Archimandrite Todor Milik and the Very Revd Dr Stevan Scott, Vol. 3 in *A Treasury of Serbian Orthodox Spirituality,* USA, no date.

Vidler, Alec R., *The Church in an Age of Revolution,* Pelican History of the Church, Vol. 5, Penguin Books, 1961.

Vlasto, A. P., *The Entry of the Slavs into Christendom,* Cambridge, 1970.

Ware, Timothy, *The Orthodox Church,* Penguin Books, Revised Edition, 1997.

West, Rebecca, *Black Lamb and Grey Falcon,* Papermac Edition, London, 1982.

Wilkinson, Alan, *The Community of the Resurrection: A Centenary History,* London, SCM Press, 1992.

INTRODUCTION

George Bell and Nikolai Velimirović were near-contemporaries, and had an almost identical lifespan. Both were men of exceptional ability, highly educated, and destined to achieve high office and eminence in their respective Churches.

Nikolai Velimirović was the elder by just over two years. He was born on December 23rd 1880 in the village of Lelić, near Valjevo in Serbia. After his early education in his native village he attended a *gimnazija* (high school) and seminary in Belgrade. He continued his theological studies in Russia, and later in the Old Catholic Theological Faculty in the University of Berne in Switzerland, where he was awarded a doctorate for a dissertation on the Resurrection *(Die Auferstehung)*. He also spent some time studying Philosophy in Germany, according to an autobiographical passage in a sermon preached in London in 1927. In 1910 he paid a short visit to England after which he returned to Belgrade, was professed as a hieromonk[1], and became a teacher in the Theological Faculty.

George Kennedy Allen Bell was born on February 4th 1883, the eldest son of the vicar of Hayling Island in Hampshire. He was educated at Westminster School and Christ Church, Oxford, where he won a classical scholarship. In April, 1906 he entered Wells Theological College and was ordained deacon in June, 1907, and priest in September, 1908. After working as a curate in Leeds parish church for two years he returned to Oxford in October 1910 as a 'Clerical Student'; possibly at this time he was considering a career as an academic theologian. However he did not pursue this idea further; in August, 1914, just after the outbreak of the First World War, he accepted an invitation to become one

---

1. A monk in Priest's Orders, a necessary condition for being ordained as a bishop in the Serbian Orthodox Church.

of the chaplains of the Archbishop of Canterbury, Randall Davidson, and remained in this post until 1924. 'For nearly half a century', writes his biographer, 'from his appointment as chaplain to Archbishop Davidson in 1914 to his resignation of the see of Chichester in 1958, George Bell was never far from the centre of Anglican ecclesiastical life and administration ...'[2]

There is no record of when George Bell and Nikolai Velimirović first met. However, this could easily have happened in connection with one of Fr Nikolai's tasks while he was in England, which was to supervise the arrangements for Serbian refugee theological students to continue their studies in England. This brought him into contact with the Archbishop of Canterbury, whose approval was necessary. Whatever the exact date of their first meeting, it was the circumstances of the First World War which drew Fr Nikolai and George Bell together; and it was then that the seed was planted of a close and lifelong friendship - a friendship which was the more remarkable because of the long periods of separation between the two friends, notably before and during the Second World War. The story of this friendship is told in the following pages.

---

2. R. C. D. Jasper, *George Bell: Bishop of Chichester*, (OUP 1967), p. 1.

I: THE FIRST WORLD WAR

The earliest reference to Fr Nikolai in George Bell's voluminous papers is an entry in his diary. He did not keep a systematic journal or diary, either during the First World War or subsequently. The entries relating to the period between December 10th 1914 and August 1919 are written in a hard-back notebook which forms Vol. 247 of his collected papers. However there are considerable gaps, and for the year 1917 there are no entries after March 15th. The entry referring to Fr Nikolai is dated February 16th, 1917, and runs as follows:

> *In the afternoon I had an interesting talk with Fr Nikolai and twenty other Serbs in an Indian restaurant (? Haymarket). Interesting talk about England and the Church of England. The English say they are interested in all things. The subject of the conversation was life. What's life? Anything ... The Ch[urch] of England was one of the protest forces in the recovery of the world. Because spiritual and liberal, with an organisation, but a loose organisation. Greatly interested also in the Church and State report. One of the Serbs, a doctor (of letters!). The other an interpreter of Meštrović who is now doing Christian sculpture. M. is of the world, not Serbian: like Shakespeare or Dante. His Crucifixion in South Kensington has the figure of a dead Jesus, but his Christ will be shown as God.*[3]

The Croatian sculptor, Ivan Meštrović, who was in London at that time, had an exhibition of his work in the Victoria and Albert Museum, which George Bell had evidently attended. He was favourably disposed towards the Serbs, and closely involved with the 'Yugoslav Committee' in London, which was working to establish a united South Slav state after the war.[4]

---

3. *Bell Papers*, vol. 247, ff. 55-56.
4. See Hugh and Christopher Seton-Watson, *The Making of a New Europe*, p.146, note 39.

At the time of the meeting described above, Fr Nikolai was thirty-seven, and George Bell was thirty-five. He was then working as one of the chaplains of the Archbishop of Canterbury (Randall Davidson) and living in Lambeth Palace. This passage in his diary suggests that he and Fr Nikolai were already well-acquainted.[5]

The atmosphere of the social gathering in the Indian restaurant is vividly conveyed: young people happily engaging in stimulating each other as they explore their different cultural backgrounds. It seems indeed to be far removed from the sombre background of the First World War. But this cannot have been absent from Fr Nikolai's mind, since the sufferings of his native land were the reason for his being in England at that time. In the autumn of 1915, Serbia had been invaded for the third time, on this occasion by the German army. The Serbs were already weakened as a result of losses in previous campaigns, and by a serious typhus epidemic during the winter of 1914-15; and their situation was made even more difficult by the entry into the war, on the German side, of their old enemy Bulgaria. By November 1915, the Serbian army was trapped in the plain of Kosovo, the scene of the defeat of the Serbs by an Ottoman Turkish army in 1389. Rather than surrender to the Germans, the remains of the Serbian army retreated through the mountains of Montenegro and Albania to the Adriatic coast. Eventually, the survivors of this epic journey, made under appalling conditions, found a refuge on the island of Corfu; later, units of the Serbian army were able to join the allies on the Salonika Front in 1917, and ultimately to re-enter their homeland.

It was in these circumstances that Fr Nikolai was sent, first to America and then to England, as a sort of ambassador extraordinary for his defeated country. His exceptional talent for languages made him particularly suitable for this task: he was fluent in

---

5. This is also indicated in an earlier passage in George Bell's Diary. (See *Bell Papers,* Vol. 247, f. 52).

Russian, French, English and German; he was also a very eloquent preacher, able to move an audience deeply even when speaking a foreign language. In the late summer of 1915, he visited America and travelled extensively through the USA, lecturing and preaching in several major cities.[6] His visit was very successful, and resulted in the despatch of over 20,000 volunteers of Slav origin to fight in Europe, most of whom eventually reached the Salonika Front. He also raised large sums of money to provide much-needed humanitarian aid for his fellow-countrymen in occupied Serbia. An interesting by-product of this visit was the contact he made with the American Episcopalian Church, which, until that time (according to one of its clergy), 'had viewed with remoteness the "exotic Eastern Orthodox Faith" '.

By the autumn of 1915, Fr Nikolai was in London, attached to the Serbian Legation. One of his first actions was to enlist the help of R. W. Seton-Watson, a well-known writer on Central and Eastern Europe, who was firmly committed both to the need to help and support Serbia in her present extremity, and also to the so-called 'Yugoslav Idea', which envisaged the eventual reunion of all the South Slavs still under foreign rule. On October 16th, Fr Nikolai wrote to him the following letter:

> *Serbia fought and died once for Christianity and civilisation. It was before five hundred years.*[7] *Serbia did always her duty, most devout and unselfish. The Serbian soldiers are now doing their sacred duty, and looking to the Leader-nation of Christianity and civilisation; they greet this island with the words:* morituri te salutant. *Will England send a help to Serbia? Serbia is not fighting only for Serbia but at the same time for India and Egypt. She is not fighting at this*

---

6. For an account of this visit, see Irinej Mirko Dobrijević, *Bishop Nicholai Velimirović. A contemporary Orthodox Witness,* Serbian Studies, *(Journal of the North American Society for Serbian Studies),* Vol.10/2 (1996).

7. Fr Nikolai is referring here to the Serbian resistance to the advance of the Ottoman Turkish armies into south-east Europe during the later decades of the fourteenth century.

*moment for a greater Serbia but for a greater world, for a
greater humanity and Christianity. I speak perhaps the last
cry of the dying Serbia: come and help us, you, the most
Christian people of the world. Remember your duty before
God! We are your unique friends between Hamburg and
Bagdad.* Drang nach Osten *is at its beginning. God's and your
cause is at stake.*[8]

In fact, Seton-Watson had already tried to persuade the British
government to send military help to Serbia, but without success.[9]

The story of Fr Nikolai's involvement with different people
who were working, in various ways, to promote the Serbian cause
lies outside the scope of this study.[10] However, one particular event
does deserve to be mentioned, because of its unusual character:
the celebration of *Vidovdan,* the anniversary of the Serbian
defeat by the Turks at the Battle of Kosovo in 1389; this was the
military defeat which subsequent legend transmuted into a spiritual victory.[11] *Vidovdan* (St Vitus Day), normally observed on
June 28th, could not be celebrated in occupied Serbia, but it was
celebrated in London. A special Kosovo committee was set up,
under the chairmanship of Dr. Elsie Inglis, who had spent
some time in Serbia as leader of a medical relief team during
the typhus epidemic. A massive publicity campaign was mounted:
a number of English writers, and also Serbs living in London,
wrote articles and translated texts which stressed the importance
of the 'Kosovo Legend' in keeping alive the spirit of the nation
during its present adversity. These were subsequently published
in book form, in 1917. R. W. Seton-Watson (one of the secretaries
of the committee) composed a special address for school-

---

8. R.W Seton-Watson, *Correspondence,* Vol. I, p. 161.
9. *The Making of a New Europe,* p. 147.
10. For details of this, see *ibid.,* pp. 163-4; 174-5; and 221-24.
11. For a detailed study of the development and significance of the Kosovo legend, see
    Thomas A. Emmert, *Serbian Golgotha, Kosovo 1389,* (1990).

children, which was read out in more than twenty thousand schools on June 28th. It was also intended to hold a special Service of Intercession for Serbia in St. Paul's Cathedral; however this was postponed, for political reasons, since June 28th was the anniversary of the assassination of Archduke Franz Ferdinand in Sarajevo in 1914. The service was therefore postponed until July 7th.

R.W. Seton-Watson described it in a letter to his wife May:

The Archbishop (of Canterbury) played up and practically blessed Jugoslavia. The choir and organ were of course quite perfect, and the Serbian anthem sung to great effect at the end, once over the organ and then two verses sung by the 300 boys ... Fr Nikolai V. in his cope took his place in the procession, and Mrs Inge (wife of the Dean) told your mother that it was the highest place of honour ever accorded to a foreign ecclesiastic in the cathedral ...[12]

It would seem that the usually cautious Archbishop Randall Davidson did allow himself to show some enthusiasm on this occasion; at any rate this was the impression of the writer of the letter.

Fr Nikolai continued his efforts to promote the Serbian cause in England, both by writing and speaking; and a number of short works written by him in English at this time have survived.[13] He also took part in a series of lectures entitled *Five Lectures on Russian and Serbian Religion* delivered at St Margaret's, Westminster, during March and April, 1916; the first two were given by the writer Stephen Graham, the remaining three by Fr Nikolai. Each lecture was accompanied by a short service, with music taken from Russian sources.[14]

---

12. See *The Making of a New Europe*, p. 175
13. See Appendix I, p. 101ff.
14. See *Randall Davidson Papers*, Vol. 520, ff. 78-84. Fr Nikolai's lectures were subsequently published in pamphlet form under the title *Sermons Suggested by the War* (1916). See Appendix I.

7

There was no doubt as to Fr Nikolai's unusual ability and effectiveness as a preacher; but this activity did raise a problem of protocol for the Church of England establishment; namely, in what particular part of an Anglican Church could Fr Nikolai preach, as a member of a different Church? In a reply to a request for clarification on this point from the Bishop of London, the Archbishop of Canterbury replied, on December 5th, 1915:

> *I cannot see that we can allow a Serbian priest to celebrate (the Liturgy) in our church unless the authority given him had the endorsement, overt or tacit, of the bishops generally. With regard to preaching, the matter is less grave ecclesiastically, and my personal feeling would be that I should not, as Archbishop of Canterbury, do anything to hamper a Diocesan Bishop who himself wished to allow this remarkable man to address a gathering of people, say, in the nave of one of our churches, by a sort of religious lecture on Serbia. To place him officially in the pulpit is quite another matter ...*[15]

Later he amplifies this statement with the following comment:

> *It would not be difficult to raise a storm from our more Protestant friends, corresponding to what our advanced friends have said about Protestant sectarians in our pulpits.*

As has already been mentioned, one of Fr Nikolai's activities while he was in England during the First World War was making arrangements for Serbian ordinands who had managed to escape to England to continue their studies. Indeed, according to George Bell, he was the originator of the scheme, which brought him into personal contact with Archbishop Randall Davidson. In his biography of Randall Davidson, George Bell writes:

---

15. *Davidson Papers*, Vol. 520, f. 71

An interesting plan for helping the Serbian students took shape this year [1917]. It sprang out of the terrible needs of a stricken country from which multitudes had been driven by invading troops. The Archbishop of Belgrade (Dimitri) was himself in exile (in Corfu) with large numbers of priests. One of these, Fr Nikolai Velimirović, a very remarkable man, proposed that the Church of England should help selected Serbian students, most of them young seminarists whose theological work had been interrupted by the war, to complete their training in certain English colleges under the supervision of Serbian priests.[16]

Actually Fr Nikolai had not taken part in the retreat to Corfu (as George Bell implies here); he was in America in the summer and early autumn of 1915, and after that in London. When he gave a lecture at King's College, London, in January 1920, the Vice-Chancellor of London University said, in the course of his introductory speech:

Before the retreat, Bishop Nikolai Velimirović would have preferred to stay with his countrymen, but duty called him to England and America to plead their cause.[17]

Another person interested in helping these students was Fr Walter Frere CR, then Superior of the Community of the Resurrection in Mirfield, who had extensive contacts with Russian and Serbian Orthodox churchmen as a result of his liturgical researches. Under the date January 11th, 1917, the Chapter minutes of the Community contain the following entry:

1. To receive 12 Serbians, preferably students, if possible to include a priest or deacon, as our guests without payment for this year, 1917;

---

16. G. K. A. Bell, *Randall Davidson, Archbishop of Canterbury,* (2nd edition, 1938, p. 844. This extract has the validity of original source material, since Bell is writing here from his own experience.

17. See *The Spiritual Rebirth of Europe* (1920), p. 16.

2. To keep them until they have learnt sufficient English to go to Oxford, when they will return to us during the vacation;

3. To exchange our guests, so that they may have some share in our life.[18]

The Archbishop, though sympathetic, was, as always, cautious, and concerned about ecclesiastical protocol; in particular he did not wish to give the scheme his official approval without a clear authorization from the Serbian Archbishop. However, Fr Nikolai somehow managed to cut through the Gordian knot, as the following letter from him to George Bell (dated June 15th, 1917) indicates:

I think you have to deal with the Serbian students as with refugees who ask for your help, material and spiritual. The letter of the Archbishop asking for the help of the Serbian Church includes the spiritual help of the Serbian candidates for priesthood. The Roman Catholics would not ask for absolute clearness and preciseness. His Grace the Archbishop of Canterbury has enough ground to help Serbia in any way he wishes. As to details, I am here in London to supply them - to explain. The general idea and apply is given already by the Archbishop of Serbia.

We have got now 11 Serbian students of theology. They are a very good material. All the responsibility for any action I will take upon myself. Either the Church will awake this year or never. It is an exceptional time ... Just as you do not ask anybody in the world whether to help materially the Serbians, so why should you ask anyone to help them spiritually? Yet, our Archbishop agrees, quite. But he can't tell it quite clearly, as he desires.[19]

---

18. I am indebted to Fr Clifford Green CR for this information. See also Alan Wilkinson, *The Community of the Resurrection. A Community History,* p. 145.
19. George Bell, *Randall Davidson,* p. 846.

Bell continues:

> *The Archbishop saw Fr Nikolai, who called himself 'Your Grace's minor brother in Christ', and accepted a clear written statement from him as the Archbishop of Belgrade's accredited representative.*

Once the Archbishop's approval had been secured, a Serbian Church Students Aid Council was established, under the Chairmanship of Canon Carnegie, Rector of St Margaret's Westminster. There was also an academic committee, including the Oxford Regius Professors of Divinity, Hebrew, Pastoral Theology and Ecclesiastical History. This committee, in conjunction with Fr Nikolai, decided on the specific courses of study to be followed by the students - which were not all the same. Most of the students were attached to St Stephen's House, Oxford.[20]

It was presumably at this period of their lives, towards the end of the First World War, that George Bell and Fr Nikolai became close personal friends. A remark in a later letter of Bell's suggests that he took a personal interest in Fr Nikolai's writings at this time, and helped him by reading his proofs. It was also a bond between them that they both admired Archbishop Randall Davidson, and were strongly influenced by him at this stage of their careers. In a letter to Bell written many years later, Fr Nikolai, then Bishop Nikolai, wrote:

As you remember, we both, as young priests, grew and for years developed our character under the guidance of that wonderful Christian wizard, the late Archbishop Randall. God rest his soul.[21]

---

20. Details of this project, with the names of the students and the courses they followed, (including titles of B. Litt. theses) can be found in the *Douglas Papers,* Vol. 51, ff. 354-7. See also George Bell's comments in *Randall Davidson,* p. 847.

21. From a letter written by Bishop Nikolai in 1946, when he was living in America *(Bell Papers,* Vol. 190, f. 143).

Fr Nikolai had many other friends and admirers in England; however (as their subsequent correspondence shows) it was with George Bell that he formed the closest bond.

By 1918, Fr Nikolai had become a well-known personality in Anglican ecclesiastical circles, much admired for his eloquent preaching, ardent patriotism and charismatic personality; also, his interest in and affection for the Church of England were much appreciated. It was felt that there should be some kind of official recognition of these sentiments, especially as it was thought that he might soon be leaving London to pay a second visit to America. (In fact this visit was postponed, and did not take place until 1921).[22] His chief advocate in this matter was the Reverend H. J. Fynes-Clinton, an Anglican priest of what Archbishop Randall Davidson described as 'advanced churchmanship' (his favourite designation of Anglo-Catholicism). Fr Fynes-Clinton was very interested in strengthening the connection between the Church of England and the Orthodox Churches, and had recently founded the Anglican and Eastern Churches Association. He was also involved in the arrangements for looking after the Serbian ordinands, and helping to organise their accommodation and provide for their material needs.

His first suggestion, put forward in a letter addressed to one of the Archbishop's chaplains (possibly George Bell), was that the Archbishop should recommend Fr Nikolai for a Lambeth D.D. He said that he did not wish to 'press the matter'; but he thought that the Archbishop ought to know that Fr Nikolai would probably soon be leaving for America, and that 'his leaving England might be considered a suitable occasion for recognition.' Later he added: 'He has been invited to lecture at some Universities in the States; and it would be a pity if they were the first to confer a degree on him.'[23]

---

22. See Dobrijević, *op.cit.* pp. 200-201.
23. *Davidson Papers*, Vol. 520, f. 89 (a letter from Fynes-Clinton, in almost illegible handwriting).

Unfortunately it was impossible to carry out this suggestion, because a Lambeth doctorate could only be awarded to a British subject; this was explained in a reply to Fynes-Clinton's letter:

The Archbishop, as you know, has the highest possible opinion of Fr Nikolai, and it would be great pleasure for him to give such tokens not only of his respect but the respect of many churchmen in England whom Fr Nikolai has impressed. But we find that the Act of Parliament passed in the time of Henry VIII, under which alone the Archbishop of Canterbury has the power to give the Lambeth degree, severely restricts such degrees to British subjects.[24]

At the end of this letter, the writer (probably George Bell) asked whether 'there had been any talk of Oxford giving him an honorary degree, especially in view of the arrival of the Serbian students'. Fynes-Clinton replied that this had indeed occurred to him, and that he would approach some people in Oxford, 'unless the Archbishop would wish to do so himself; that would be more promising of success'.[25]

However, there were restrictions with regard to this suggestion also: Fr Nikolai could not be given an honorary Oxford D.D. because he was not in priest's orders in the Church of England. He would be eligible for a D.C.L., or a D.Litt.; but these degrees were not in general being awarded during the war. George Bell wrote to Canon Carnegie, the chairman of the Serbian Church Students Aid Committee, to ask for his help:

The Archbishop has asked me to write to let you know the facts,' he wrote. *'Possibly you might feel inclined to approach Dr Holland,*[26] *or some other eminent Oxford Professor or dignitary on the subject.*[27]

---

24. *Davidson Papers*, Vol. 520, ff. 92-3.
25. *Ibid*, ff. 93-4.
26. Dr. Henry Scott Holland, an eminent preacher and theologian.
27. *Davidson Papers*, Vol. 520, f. 103.

Canon Carnegie's reply, dated March 17th, 1918, was not at all encouraging; indeed it was more than a little patronising in tone:

> ... *the honour sought,* he wrote, *is a very considerable one, not to be lightly accorded. We know and appreciate Fr Nikolai's merits and powers, but he still has to 'make good' in the English academic world ... Moreover, a consideration not to be overlooked, one has to be a little careful in one's dealings with these Orientals. They are, all of them, I find, a little apt to get above themselves, and to make a larger claim for recognition than Englishmen of similar status would think of making ... this is a lesson that Fr Velimirović has not yet fully learnt, as Frere is just learning to his cost ...*[28]

In fairness to Fr Nikolai, it should be borne in mind that he had already 'made good academically' at the University of Berne, and that he was not (so far as we know) personally seeking any special academic recognition in England. However, Fynes-Clinton was not to be beaten. His final suggestion, which proved to be acceptable to all concerned, was that Fr Nikolai should be presented with a specially-designed Pectoral Cross and Chain, 'of a design which includes some symbol of its English Church origin, and of his work for reunion ...' He goes on to say:

> *The position of influence his personality and merit have gained and the work that he has done in preaching in many of our Cathedrals and Churches, in his lectures and writings, is unprecedented for an Orthodox priest in this country, and it is a matter of great satisfaction to us that he is soon to be consecrated Bishop, and that he will thus be able fully to exercise his influence in the reconstruction of the life of the Church and the country of Serbia on its liberation.* [29]

---

28. *Ibid.,* f. 105.
29. *Ibid.,* f. 107.

The minimum subscription suggested for the purchase of this cross was 7/6d, and it was to be presented by the Archbishop of Canterbury.[30]

The First World War ended with the Armistice signed on November 11th, 1918. In the same month, the Serbian army (the survivors from the retreat across the mountains) had marched into Belgrade. The following month saw the proclamation of the Kingdom of Serbs, Croats and Slovenes. Fr Nikolai was now preparing to return to his native land, as bishop-designate of the ancient see of Žiča, from which St Sava had organised the autocephalous Serbian Orthodox Church early in the thirteenth century.[31] The first phase of his connection with England, and in particular with the Church of England, was over; in future he was to pay only short visits to the country. But his friendship with George Bell, and his affection for England and its people, lasted to the end of his life.

---

30. It would be interesting to know what happened to this cross, and whether Bishop Nikolai still had it with him during his years of exile in America.
31. See A. P. Vlasto, *The Entry of the Slavs into Christendom,* (1970), pp. 221-3. Throughout his life Bishop Nikolai had a special devotion to St. Sava.

II: 1919 - 1939 (Between the Wars)

Fr Nikolai returned to the recently-established Kingdom of Serbs, Croats and Slovenes (Yugoslavia) at the end of 1918 to take up his duties as Bishop of Žiča. At the end of the following year he made his first post-war visit to England, from December 1919 to January 20th, 1920. During this visit he gave a number of lectures and sermons, the most important being a lecture at King's College London entitled *The Spiritual Rebirth of Europe;* and a sermon preached in St Paul's Cathedral on *The Principle of the Eastern Orthodox Church.* These, together with two other shorter addresses, were later published by the Faith Press under the title of *The Spiritual Rebirth of Europe.*[1] In March 1920, the *Church Times* printed a special tribute to Bishop Nikolai to celebrate this publication:

> *During the four years of the war*[2] *that he spent in England,* says the writer, *Dr Nikolai Velimirović impressed himself, his personality and his message on a very wide circle of Englishmen, so that when he returned to Serbia we were conscious of real loss. When he visited England again last December, his message seemed to have gained an additional force, naturally, since he had recovered touch with his own people, and had received the grace of consecration and assumed new responsibilities. What he said in St Paul's, at King's College and in other places lingers in our ears. That it might not fade from our memory the Faith Press has published four sermons and addresses under the title of* The Spiritual Rebirth of Europe *(1s.). It is prefaced in a few words by the Rev. J. A. Douglas. We counsel all to get this little volume, the message of one who, in the words of the*

---

1. See Appendix I, p. 104.
2. Actually Fr Nikolai spent just over three years in England during the war, from the autumn of 1915 to the end of 1918.

Vice-Chancellor of the University of London, 'not only inter-prets the mind of the Orthodox Serbs to us, but has some-thing to say which is peculiarly his own, who is not only a provoker of thought and a stimulating personality, but has the rarer gift of practical application of ideals.'[3]

It was during this visit that Bishop Nikolai wrote the first letter to George Bell which has been preserved among Bell's papers. In this letter, written from 13, Old Burlington Street and dated January 10th, 1919,[4] he says that he has been extremely busy, but he hopes to see George Bell before he leaves England at the end of the following week.

I intended to invite some 8-10 friends one day next week,' he writes. *'It would be excellent if each one of us had two Egos (though we are egoistic enough with one) one to work with and the other to be in company of one's friends. I shall let you know when we can meet.*[5]

He also thanks Bell for sending him a translated appeal from the Pope, which he says he will send to the Archbishop of Belgrade.[6]

Bishop Nikolai did not serve very long as Bishop of Žiča; in 1920 he was transferred to Ochrid, in Macedonia. Ochrid had been an ancient and prestigious diocese of the Byzantine Church, whose incumbent in the early medieval period had had the title of archbishop. The Orthodox Serbs had been under this jurisdiction until they acquired autocephalous status for the kingdom of Serbia in 1219.[7] However, the area included in this

---

3. *Douglas Papers*, Vol. 51, f. 160.
4. This should be 1920 - a mistake easily made at the beginning of a new year, and Bishop Nikolai was no doubt under pressure, as he had a very full programme.
5. *Bell Papers*, Vol. 190, f. 317.
6. I have so far been unable to trace this document.
7. See above, p. 15.

diocese when Nikolai Velimirović became its bishop had only recently been recovered from Turkish rule,[8] and most of the population were materially and culturally backward. Moreover before the development of air transport, Ochrid was very isolated even from other parts of Yugoslavia, let alone the rest of Europe. It seems a strange decision[9] to transfer to that see a man who was an accomplished linguist, and who already had a considerable reputation as a writer and a theologian; and who had during the recent war established cordial relations with the Anglican Church and won the respect and affection of some of its leaders, including the Archbishop of Canterbury. There is ample evidence in Bishop Nikolai's correspondence with George Bell and other Anglican churchmen that he found the geographical isolation of Ochrid irksome, because of the difficulty of seeing and visiting his friends; also he was deeply concerned about the extreme poverty and primitive lifestyle of most of the people to whom he been called upon to minister. On at least one occasion, he personally had a narrow escape from death at the hands of brigands.[10] On the other hand, he greatly appreciated the awe-inspiring natural beauty of his surroundings, and the peace and quiet which he was able to enjoy there; this provided inspiration for one of his finest devotional works, entitled *Prayers by the Lake*.[11] The years that Bishop Nikolai had spent in London certainly provided scope for the social side of his nature, and for his gift for friendship, and his power to stimulate others. However, although he missed his friends while he was in Ochrid, his experience there helped to develop the more contemplative aspect of his personality.

---

8. See M. Heppell and F. B. Singleton, *Yugoslavia,* pp. 131-2.

9. There is no indication in any official history as to why Bishop Nikolai was transferred from Žiča to Ochrid.

10. See *Douglas Papers,* Vol. 51, f. 183.

11. There is an English translation of this work, published in USA, under the title *Prayers by the Lake,* translated and annotated by Archimandrite Todor Milik and the Very Revd Dr Stevan Scott. Vol. 3 in the series *A Treasury of Serbian Spirituality* (no date given).

Although much of his time was spent in routine administration and caring for his flock, Bishop Nikolai was also concerned about ecclesiastical affairs outside his diocese. One of the first of these was a request, in 1920, from a group of reformist Czech Catholics, to amalgamate with the Serbian Orthodox Church;[12] this involved complicated negotiations, which he later described in a letter to George Bell as a 'boiling kettle'.[13] He was also involved (or at any rate keenly interested) in a crisis in the Ecumenical Patriarchate of Constantinople.[14] And like George Bell, he was interested in the preliminary negotiations to set up a World Council of Churches, although it would seem that he did not take a very active part in these.

George Bell, during the immediate post-war years, continued to work as chaplain to the Archbishop of Canterbury (Randall Davidson), during which time he lived in Lambeth Palace.[15] In 1924, he received his first senior appointment in the Church of England, as Dean of Canterbury Cathedral; then in 1929 he was consecrated Bishop of Chichester. In both these posts he showed himself to be a man of versatile gifts and tireless energy. During this period in Canterbury, he broke new ground by seeking to bring the arts - especially music, poetry and drama - into the service of the Church, and he continued this activity after he became Bishop of Chichester.[16] He was also much involved in inter-Church relations, at various levels; and after Hitler's rise to power in Germany he became deeply involved in the problems of the Lutheran Church in that country; he was particularly concerned about the struggle between the so-called German State Church, which supported the Nazi government, and the Confessing Church, which fought a losing battle to maintain its

12. See Appendix II, p. 105.
13. See below, p. 21.
14. *Douglas Papers*, Vol. 51, f. 169.
15. R. C. D. Jasper, *George Bell*, p. 27.
16. *Ibid.*, pp. 40-45; 121-129.

freedom.[17] He also took an active part in the Life and Work movement, and the preparatory work which eventually led to the establishment of the World Council of Churches.[18] And as though all this was not enough, he found time and energy to write a monumental biography of his early mentor, Archbishop Randall Davidson.[19]

Apart from their mutual interest in the Life and Work movement, George Bell and Bishop Nikolai pursued different activities and wrote on different subjects during the inter-war years; what they had in common was their tremendous drive and energy, and their commitment to whatever it was that they were doing. In view of this, it is perhaps surprising that they found the time to write to each other at all; less surprising, and more interesting, that their correspondence is primarily personal ... Bishop Nikolai's letters to Canon J. A. Douglas (after 1926, Secretary to the Church of England Council for Foreign Relations) throw interesting light on what he was doing; but when he wrote to George Bell, he revealed more of his thoughts and his inner life, as the following letter shows:

November 24th, 1921,
Ochrida

My dear friend,
         Peace be with you.
It is a real shame that I write to you so belated. You asked me in your latest letter about the chequoslovak [sic] *question, and I was then in the boiling kettle of it. Tremendous mani-festations and ceremonies crushed me like an atom. Now I am, thank God, on the peaceful lake of Ochrida. It is almost the peace beyond understanding. I have been writing* Prayers by the Lake. *I am not like our friend the Rev. Quick who is*

---

17. *Ibid.,* pp. 100-118.

18. *Ibid.,* Chapter 6; see also G. K. A. Bell, *The Kingship of Christ,* Chapters 1 and 2.

19. This was originally published in 1935, in two volumes; a second one-volume edition appeared in 1938, and a third edition, with some additional material, in 1952. See Jasper, *George Bell,* pp. 76-78.

fond of systematic theology,[20] *for which is necessary an acute brain, and brain alone. I for myself am afraid of things done by the brain alone, because the brain rushes too much towards the Tree of Knowledge. I am fond of the Tree of Life, and in order to arrive at this tree one needs three legs: brain, heart and soul. In these my prayers I am trying to walk on three legs, which is of course very hard to do for our generation, trained to walk on one leg only - the brain.* Then he adds (perhaps not wishing to appear critical): *May the Lord bless our friend Quick.*[21]

Later in this letter, he writes at some length on the current situation in Russia, where he says: 'Do as much as you can for Russia. In a year or so Russia will be quite changed, and very wonderful. Her enemies will be ashamed.'

The next letter from Bishop Nikolai preserved among Bell's papers was written some two and a half years later: a letter of congratulation on his appointment as Dean of Canterbury, dated August 19th, 1924.[22] He begins with the traditional Orthodox Easter greeting: 'Christ is risen!' then goes on to apologise for not having written earlier. 'It is hardly my fault,' he writes, 'though I am full of faults and even sins - Rev. Douglas informed me about it only some few days ago.'[23] After commenting on the historical importance of Canterbury in the history of the English Church, he says:

---

20. Oliver Quick was also chaplain to the Archbishop of Canterbury at the same time as George Bell, until he became an army chaplain in 1917. He later became well known as a writer of theological books.

21. *Bell Papers,* Vol. 200, f. 208.

22. *ibid,* Vol. 200, f. 208.

23. These words suggest that George Bell and Bishop Nikolai had not been in regular communication for some time.

Being under the fatherly hand of the Archbishop of Canterbury for such a long time,[24] *you have gone through a most valuable school where one has much, much to learn. I am sure that you will all that accumulated knowledge and piety utilise to the best as Dean of Canter[bury].*[25]

The next exchange of letters between the two friends took place in 1926. This arose from a suggestion that Bishop Nikolai might write, in English, a book on the Orthodox Church suitable for the general reader, to form part of a series being planned by the publishing firm Methuen. George Bell had been asked by Dr L. P. Jacks, (then Principal of Manchester College, Oxford, and editor of the *Hibbert Journal*) to suggest someone to write a book of about 50,000 words on 'The Faith of the Greek Church'.[26]

Dr Jacks asked me to recommend a writer on the Greek Church, he wrote, *and I replied by asking him whether he wanted a historical, and, so to speak, objective account from the outside, or an account from the inside, giving the reader the atmosphere of the Orthodox Church with a sufficient regard for history, but making the spirit of Orthodoxy the primary concern ... If he desired the latter there was no one whom I would rather see writing such a book as yourself. He was most decidedly in favour of a book from the inside ... Now I hope very much that you will see your way to accepting*

---

24. A reference to Bell's period of service as chaplain to Archbishop Randall Davidson.

25. Admiration for Archbishop Randall Davidson, and an awareness of having been strongly influenced by him during a formative period of their lives, was part of the close bond between George Bell and Bishop Nikolai, which the latter recalled in a letter to Bell many years later (see above, p. 11).

26. The term 'Greek (or Greek Orthodox) Church' was often used in English (and still is) to describe all the Orthodox Churches; this is a misleading description, since it fails to indicate one of the important characteristics of Orthodoxy, namely the organisation of separate autonomous Churches.

this invitation. It is really important that there should be a first-rate book in English giving the character and meaning of the Orthodox Church in an authoritative and attractive way.[27] *Please tell me that you will consent ...* [28]

At the end of this letter, Bell says that he would be happy to help with such a book in any way he could, including reading the proofs. 'I have read your proofs before,' he wrote,' and it would be a privilege to do it again.'[29]

Over two months passed without him receiving a reply to this letter: an awkward situation! So on June 8th, 1926 he wrote to Bishop Nikolai again on the same subject, and pointed out as tactfully as possible that he felt he ought not to keep Dr Jacks waiting any longer, 'as he wants to get his plans forward'.[30] This time he did get a reply, dated June 12th, probably written immediately after Bishop Nikolai had received his letter.

I was told that Dr Jacks belongs to the Unitarians,' wrote Bishop Nikolai. *Therefore my hesitation. Even now I don't know what to answer. Are not the Unitarians the same in doctrine as the Moslems and the Jews? How could they then understand a complicated system of grace like the ancient Church of the East? Our doctrine would be for them either wholly new or wholly old one. In both cases they will not like it. But if you tell me to write it for you, I will do it, and you will give it to who you want. Though I am living in a secluded jungle, I am occupied enough.*

---

27. Although there was at this time a fairly considerable corpus of scholarly work on the Orthodox churches, notably, the writings of such pioneers as William Palmer and John Mason Neale, there was as yet no short 'authoritative and attractive book' such as Methuen evidently had in mind.

28. *Bell Papers,* Vol. 190, f. 211 (a typed copy of Bell's letter to Bishop Nikolai).

29. See above, p. 11.

30. *Bell Papers,* Vol. 200, f. 212.

He then goes on to say that he does not really see the need for such a book on 'the religion of the Christian East', as it is already 'marvellously expressed in the Holy Fathers of the Church.' He ends his letter: 'But if you ask me to do it, and you promise to pray for me - then I will try.'[31]

Bell replied to this letter on June 21st, 1926:

I am deeply grateful for your letter of June 12th, received today,' he wrote. *'Dr Jacks is a Unitarian, but his religious belief is very, very different from that of Moslems and Jews. And indeed he is accounted a religious leader of great force and value. In any case I am very sure that you and I will be in thorough accord and it shall be through me that your book is written. I most gratefully accept what you say and ask you to write it for me, and I will give it to whom I wish.* He adds, as a comment on Bishop Nikolai's remark about the Fathers: ... *very many who would read such a book as you would write interpreting the Fathers would not be able to read the Holy Fathers for themselves.*[32]

From the content of these letters, it would seem that George Bell had a deep understanding of the 'spirit of Orthodoxy' and that Bishop Nikolai was aware of this. There is no hint of this in Jasper's biography of George Bell; but Bell does speak of it him-self in his book *The Kingship of Christ*. In the section entitled 'Orthodox and Protestant' he says:

But in spite of these serious doctrinal differences, especially in the concept of the nature of the Church and worship, and

---

31. *Ibid.*, f. 213. As far as I know, this projected book was never written.

32. Translations of the works of the Fathers, both Eastern and Western, were available in English at this time; however Bell was probably right in assuming that people who would read a short book on Orthodoxy by Bishop Nikolai would not themselves read the Fathers.

of the means of grace, not only an understanding but a closer contact between these two great Christian traditions is entirely possible ... I say all this with full confidence, after discussion with Orthodox friends for many years, both before and since the Second World War. And I have been much helped for my present purpose by advice, both in conversation and writing ... from Professor Hamilcar Alivasatos, the great theologian of Athens.[33]

Although Bell specifically mentions Professor Alivasatos here, there can be little doubt that his earlier conversations with Fr Nikolai during the First World War had also played a part in developing his understanding of Orthodoxy.

Bell's letter to Bishop Nikolai of June 21st, 1926 is the last in their correspondence until after the Second World War. The lack of communication during the war is, of course, understandable, but less so for the long period between 1926 and 1939. Fortunately, the *Douglas Papers* contain considerable information about Bishop Nikolai's activities during this time, including a detailed account of his visit to London in 1927, when he and George Bell met again.

During the years immediately after the First World War, the two friends were frustrated in their attempts to meet personally, though there was clearly a strong desire on both sides that they should do so. At the end of his long letter to George Bell written from Ochrid in November, 1921, Bishop Nikolai says:

I have been chosen as a delegate bishop for Serbian Church in America. And probably, if God wills, I may meet you next spring in the Lambeth again on my way to America.[34]

---

33. *The Kingship of Christ,* pp. 60-61.
34. *Bell Papers,* Vol. 190, f. 321.

However, the meeting in London did not take place; in a subsequent letter to George Bell, obviously written in a hurry, with no address or date, Bishop Nikolai says:

> *Strange as it may appear to you and me is that we are not going to meet this time. When you are reading this note I shall be on the train going away from England. I had this time to be here quite incognito. There are many reasons for that, one of which is that the Eastern bishops, (especially I myself) do come very often to this country ... Now I promise you that I will gladly stop in London on my way back*[35] *and do all the visits you wish me to do.*

At the end of this short letter he says that his *Prayers by the Lake* have now been published in Belgrade.[36]

There is something mysterious about this proposed visit to America in 1922; and there is no indication that it ever did include a meeting between Bishop Nikolai and George Bell. Irinej Dobrijević describes Bishop Nikolai's second visit to the USA under the year 1921, and says that this was the result of invitations from a number of American universities, and that he gave some 140 lectures and sermons in different cathedrals and universities; also that he established a separate Serbian Orthodox diocese for North America, and was its titular bishop until 1923. He says nothing about any visit in 1922.[37]

---

35. Presumably Bishop Nikolai means that he hopes to see George Bell on his way back from America.

36. *Bell Papers*, Vol. 190, f. 322. Bishop Nikolai does not explain why he would have to visit London 'incognito'; possibly the reason had to do with ecclesiastical politics within the Serbian Orthodox Church.

37. See Irinej Dobrijević, *Bishop Nicholai Velimirović. A Contemporary Orthodox Witness*, pp. 201-205. There seems to be some discrepancy in connection with the dates here. According to Bishop Nikolai's earlier letter to George Bell, he was expecting to visit America early in 1922; however Dobrijević dates this visit January - July 1921 (possibly another example of a 'slip of the pen' on the part of Bishop Nikolai).

The circumstances of the next attempt to arrange a meeting were more straightforward. On March 7th, 1925, Bell wrote to Bishop Nikolai saying that he and Mrs Bell, together with Canon Quick and his wife, were planning to visit Dalmatia at the end of April, after spending ten days in Venice.

> *Alas, we shall only be there for a fortnight,* he writes, *as I have to be back by Saturday, May 16th. I know that Ochrid is a long way from the Adriatic. But I am wondering whether there would be any chance of our meeting in any of the places I have mentioned (Spoleto, Ragusa, Cattaro)*[38] *or some place near. And I do not like to come to any part of Yugoslavia, however remote, without letting you know.*[39]

Bishop Nikolai replied to this letter on April 20th, 1925.

It is with mixed joy and pain that I took knowledge of your arrival in this country, he wrote. *With joy, because you have come nearer me, and with pain, because I am afraid it will be impossible for me to come and meet you.* [40]

Not only, he goes on to say, because the journey would be 'an awful time-eater',[41] but also because he had to act as chairman of a committee set up to prepare a memorial celebration in honour of an early medieval Serbian ruler, Prince Vladimir, who met a martyr's death near Ochrid in 1015.[42] He asked, very tentatively, whether his English friends could perhaps visit Ochrid?

---

38. Bell uses the Italian form of the names of towns now better known by their Croatian form: i.e. Split, Dubrovnik, and Kotor.
39. *Bell Papers,* Vol. 200, f. 209.
40. *Ibid.,* f. 210.
41. Bishop Nikolai says that the journey from Ochrid to Dubrovnik would take him five days. A direct flight today takes just over two hours!
42. See Voyeslav Yanich, *Lives of the Serbian Saints,* Eastern Orthodox Books (Willits. California, 1974), pp. 1-5. This is a short account of the death of Prince Vladimir, probably early in the eleventh century. According to this story, he seems to have been the victim of a political murder, rather than a Christian martyr. It is written in conventional hagiographical style, and might well be of ancient origin. Unfortunately there is no indication of the original text on which this narrative is based.

We have old churches, he says, *though not as gorgeous as those in Dalmatia - and a beautiful lake.*[43]

If this is not possible, perhaps they could meet in Skoplje or Belgrade.[44] In any case he advises his friends to visit a number of places of historical interest which would be reasonably accessible from Dalmatia:

Try from Spalato [Split] to motor to the Serb monastery of Krka,[45] *and going from Castel Nuovo [Kastel Novi], near Split to Cattaro [Kotor] to see the monastery of Savina;*[46] *and from Cattaro by all means go to Cetinje.*[47] *I have written about you to Bishop Kiril in Cattaro, Bishop Danil in Šibenica,*[48] *and to Metropolitan Gavril in Cetinje.*[49]

It was no doubt disappointing to both George Bell and Bishop Nikolai that they were unable to meet when Bell visited Yugoslavia in 1925; however a favourable opportunity for a reunion presented itself some two and a half years later, in November 1927. In August that year Bishop Nikolai was once more invited to America,[50] this time as the guest of the American Yugoslav Society, the Institute of Politics in

---

43. Rebecca West says that 'the old town of Ochrid on its hill is stuck as thickly with churches as a pomander with cloves' *(Black Lamb and Grey Falcon,* p. 709). The most important are the Church of Holy Wisdom, Sveti Kliment (St Clement) and St John Bigorski, on a promontory overlooking the lake.

44. *Bell Papers,* Vol. 200, f. 210.

45. An Orthodox monastery situated on the banks of Riva Krka in northern Dalmatia; its library contained a rich collection of Slavonic manuscripts of glagolitic origin. (See A. P. Vlasto, *The Entry of the Slavs into Christendom,* pp. 201-205). Though originally under Roman jurisdiction, it also had an Orthodox monastery with a considerable collection of Cyrillic manuscripts. I understand that this monastery was badly damaged during the recent fighting in Yugoslavia.

46. An Orthodox monastery on the southern Adriatic coast, at the mouth of the Bay of Kotor (Boka Kotorska).

47. The capital of Montenegro; there is an ancient Orthodox monastery there, with a considerable collection of manuscripts.

48. A town on the central Dalmatian coast, with a mixed Catholic and Orthodox population.

49. *Bell Papers,* Vol. 200, f. 210.

50. Dobrijević, *Bishop Nicholai Velimirović. A Contemporary Orthodox Witness,* p. 206.

Williamstown, (Massachussets), and the Carnegie Endowment for International Peace. As on his previous visits, he travelled around and lectured and preached in a number of places, including both Orthodox and Episcopalian churches.[51] On his way back to Yugoslavia he spent ten days in London, where his programme included lunch with the Archbishop of Canterbury[52] (Cosmo Gordon Lang), and a visit as guest preacher to St Luke's, Camberwell (where Canon Douglas was the incumbent) and dinner as the guest of the Nikean Club, where George Bell (now Dean of Canterbury) was to take the chair. The details of this visit were fully reported in the *Church Times,* and are of special interest because of the light they throw on both Bishop Nikolai's inner life at that time and his views on current problems of secular and ecclesiastical life.

The visit to St Luke's, Camberwell was scheduled for the evening of Sunday, November 13th; apparently one reason for this visit was to enable Bishop Nikolai to see the Chapel of Unity in this church, recently dedicated by Bishop Gore.[53] The visit was fully reported in the *Church Times* as follows:

> *A remarkable sermon was preached last Sunday at Even-song at the Church of St Luke, Camberwell, concerning the funda-mentals of the Christian faith. The service followed the usual course of Evensong except that Bishop Nikolai Velimirović was met at the door by the Vicar (Canon J. A. Douglas) and a bevy of wolf cubs carrying lanterns, and was conducted to his throne in the chancel. It was all dignified and picturesque. A* Te Deum *was sung at the conclusion of the service.*[54]

---

51. Dobrijević says that Bishop Nikolai's involvement with the Serbian Orthodox Church in the United States during this visit was 'extremely limited', on account of internal dissensions within the Church.
52. See *Douglas Papers,* Vol. 51, f. 185.
53. *Ibid.,* f. 186. This visit must have given Bishop Nikolai an opportunity to see an area of London rather different from those he had seen on his previous visits.
54. *Douglas Papers,* Vol. 51, f. 197. Possibly this account was written for the *Church Times* by Canon Douglas.

It was indeed a remarkable sermon,[55] preached on a text from I John 1: 3[56] - remarkable for the range and variety of its subject matter, the intensity of thought and feeling expressed, and the challenge it presented to the listeners - though perhaps a bit above the heads of the wolf cubs.

The main theme of the sermon is that the key to the understanding of the Christian faith is not knowledge gained from books (or other sources), but personal religious experience. Bishop Nikolai's first illustration is a recollection of his own personal experience as a young man:

I remember that when I was a student of Philosophy in Germany I was very much confused by all that was written of Philosophy. I was almost on the verge of suicide, as are many young people of today, I am sorry to say. I went to Palestine, and there I went to the Monastery of the Temptation overlooking Jericho.[57] I did not go there for curiosity's sake. I saw the Master of the Monastery and he pointed to me an old man, bright and shining with faith, and I went to him and told him everything about myself. Then he smiled and said 'But your soul is starving, therefore you think of suicide. Why did you run after philosophies and human opinions? Why did you not read other people's spiritual experiences and then try to have your own experiences?' I said that I had not heard of that. He said 'Have you read the Scripture? That is the standard of spiritual experience. The first is the Scripture, and then the lives of the saints.' That saved my soul and made me an optimist in this life. Understand that all our religion is founded on experience, just as any physical science.

---

55. There is a transcript of this sermon in the *Douglas Papers,* Vol. 51, ff. 187-196.

56. *That which we have seen and heard declare we unto you , that ye may also have fellowship with us; and truly, our fellowship is with the Father, and with his Son Jesus Christ* (AV).

57. There is a space in the typescript here (f. 190), but the name of the monastery is included in the summary of the sermon published in the *Church Times.* (*Douglas Papers,* Vol. 51, f. 197).

He goes on to say:

> *Our religion is founded on spiritual experience, seen and heard as surely as any physical fact in this world. Not theory, not philosophy, not human emotions, but experience ... Our soul is the living bridge between this world and the invisible. With our soul we can be in touch with God and with His angels and with the Saints by the spiritual experience which the Saints and the Church confirmed and verified.*

He then describes a number of 'spiritual realities' which form the basis of Christian religious experience:

> *The first and greatest spiritual reality is that Christ is not dead, but is the living Lord of Glory ... The second great one is the World of Spiritual Hosts, marvels and wonderful signs, and the Glory of the Lord, the Angels, the Archangels, the myriads and myriads of those who have passed from our midst ... then there is the third spiritual reality which we are always wanting to know. Our friends who have passed from this life - they are not dead, they are living ... And there is a fourth great spiritual reality, which is going to be, and that is that God is going to judge the world. The prophetic minds of the saints, they have seen, they have verified many more spiritual realities. But if you believe, if you are sure of these four, you have heard what is joyful for you in the toils of this life.*[58]

Then he turns to contemporary society, and the dangers arising from the rejection of religious experience:

> *There are, however, people in Europe who are troubled in mind and therefore making trouble in everything. They have separated themselves from the soul of the people, God's people. They have separated themselves from the Church experiences*

---

58. *Douglas Papers*, Vol. 51, ff. 190-192.

... and they are trying to find new ways and new truths, as it were. Many of these people are leading and ruling the nations. That is the great misfortune of the times.[59]

He follows this general statement with a specific appeal to 'the youth of England.' Recalling the life and witness of the early saints of the British Isles - St Alban, St David and St Columba,[60] he says:

I assure you that nothing you will find in the history of your country is so marvellous and so wonderful as the Church of Christ which was founded by the holy men of this country.

He turns to the wider world:

People speak of the need for organisation, people speak of Church Unity, of the certainty of all Christians, of the League of Nations ... But unless we are living and practising in our lives that which our souls are living for ... we are unfit to solve any problem today. But when we are sure of our spiritual realities, then we have power, we have much, we have fitness to perform [?reform] all these great world problems.[61]

Finally he says in conclusion:

It is a great thing to be called. The people are looking to you to say what you have to say. What message do you bring to the people, and what news of Christ? No other message for the world today is expected. No other message can make the world joyful but the Christian message which will never make us ashamed.[62]

---

59. *Ibid.*, ff. 192-3.
60. The references here to St David and St Columba show that Bishop Nikolai is not thinking of England in the narrow geographical sense, but of Britain as a whole.
61. *Douglas Papers*, Vol. 51, f. 195. Bishop Nikolai was certainly interested in developing relations of fellowship between different Churches, but not in unity imposed by organisational or political means.
62. *Douglas Papers*, Vol. 51, f. 196.

The dinner at the Nikean Club[63] was held on the following Tuesday (November 16th), at the Holborn Restaurant. George Bell was in the chair, and in this capacity he proposed a toast to Bishop Nikolai, as the guest of honour, and to the reunion of Christendom.

'Dr Bell referred to the bad old times,' says the *Church Times* report, 'when Christian people gloried in their divisions. Nowadays things had completely changed round. There was hardly a Christian communion from whom they could not learn something. The real unity was one composed of faith and love. They had that night as their guest one who had played a great part in the world movement for Reunion. They welcomed him as one of the great figures of international Christianity. They welcomed him because he represented the great Orthodox Church of the East, and they welcomed him for his own sake as an old and dear friend.'

In his reply Bishop Nikolai spoke in some detail about his recent visit to America, and the impression that this had left on him.

'There were plenty of critics who found fault with America,' continued the *Church Times* report, 'but he went there looking for something to praise. He talked about his meetings with American Church leaders who had recently returned from the Faith and Order conference in Lausanne,[64] and went on to say: "Reunion would only come if they wholeheartedly desired it, without any selfish motives, and for the glory of God." '

---

63. The Nikean Club was established in 1925 (the 1,600th anniversary of the Council of Nicea in 325), for the purpose of exercising hospitality, on behalf of the Archbishop of Canterbury, to Christians belonging to non-Anglican traditions.

64. The first International Conference on Faith and Order was held in Lausanne in 1927 (see *The Kingship of Christ*, pp. 29-30).

'Finally he expressed his gratitude for what the Anglican Church had done during the First World War to help Serbian ordinands to complete their theological studies in England. With this splendid work in mind, he proposed the health of the Anglican communion.'[65]

After 1929, when George Bell became Bishop of Chichester, he too, like Bishop Nikolai, had to spend much of his time and energy on diocesan administration and related problems of pastoral care.[66] However, there was one activity in which they were both interested, and which provided at least one opportunity for a personal meeting during the years before the Second World War. This was the so-called 'ecumenical movement',[67] and particularly that aspect of it known as the Universal Christian Council for Life and Work.

George Bell had been involved with this movement, within the framework of inter-Church relations,[68] from the time of the First World War. He was a member of the editorial board of the Orthodox journal *Put* (The Way), published by the Russian Orthodox Theological Institute in Paris, and his activity in connection with this journal was much appreciated by Nicholas Berdayev.[69] In 1919, he attended the first post-war meeting of the International Committee of the World Alliance for promoting International Friendship through the Churches held at Oud Wasser; it was at this meeting that a decision was taken to hold a world conference of Churches to discuss social and moral

---

65. *Douglas Papers,* Vol. 51, f. 197.

66. See Jasper, *George Bell,* pp. 70-86.

67. In his book, *The Kingship of Christ* (1954), George Bell refers to a remark made by William Temple when he was Archbishop of Canterbury, acclaiming this 'world-wide Christian fellowship, this Ecumenical Movement, as it has been called, as the great new fact of our era' (p. 18).

68. Bell himself distinguishes between the two meanings of the word 'ecumenical', i.e. 'world-wide', and what Visser't Hooft described as 'spiritual traffic between the Churches' *(Ibid).*

69. Jasper, *George Bell,* p. 56.

questions. This conference took place in Stockholm in August 1925, under the title of the Universal Christian Council on Life and Work. Bell was a delegate at this conference, and participated actively in the drafting of its final message.[70]

Bishop Nikolai was not so much involved in these activities, nor even very well-informed about them, though the Serbian Orthodox Church supported them.[71] This was probably partly because of the remoteness of his diocese, though there may have been other reasons connected with domestic ecclesiastical politics. However, he was interested in the proposed conference at Stockholm, as can be seen from his question in a letter to Canon Douglas, dated June 22nd, 1925:

> *Now I want to ask you about the world conference of Life and Work in Stockholm this autumn. Tell me, please, is your Church going to take part in it, or is she not? And what sort of people are those who have invited all the Churches to that conference?*[72]

Bishop Nikolai did not attend this conference, though among the six hundred delegates who did there were several Orthodox, including Patriarch Photios of Alexandria and Archbishop Germanos of Thyateira.[73] However, he was present at a meeting of the executive committee of the Universal Christian Council for Life and Work which met in Novi Sad (a city on the banks of the Danube with a mixed Serbian and Hungarian population) hosted by the Orthodox Bishop of Bačka (Irinej Ćirić) whom George Bell describes as 'a saintly and devoted advocate of

---

70. *The Kingship of Christ*, p. 28; cf. Jasper, *George Bell*, pp. 61-3.
71. The Roman Catholic Church took no part in this ecumenical activity, nor did the Russian Orthodox Church; however other Orthodox Churches, especially the Greeks, did participate actively.
72. *Douglas Papers*, Vol. 51, f. 181.
73. *The Kingship of Christ*, p. 27.

Christian unity.[74] This was the last time that he and Bishop Nikolai met until after the Second World War.[75]

It is not surprising, especially in view of the geographical isolation of Ochrid, that it was difficult for the two bishops to meet personally, unless the meetings could be fitted into the framework of official engagements, such as Bishop Nikolai's visit to the USA in 1927, or George Bell's attendance at the executive committee of the Life and Work conference in Novi Sad in 1933; this was not quite so far from Ochrid as some other places which Bell visited - though Bishop Nikolai did say in a letter to Canon Douglas that it took him three days to travel to Belgrade.[76] There was no exchange of letters during this period either; or if there was, nothing of the correspondence has survived. Probably the main reason for this was that both bishops were deeply involved in a variety of activities and problems which absorbed and even exhausted their energy, but did not provide any point of contact. Commenting on George Bell's early years as Bishop of Chichester, his biographer writes:

> *But what was really astonishing was the continued width of his interests and his capacity for work. Over and above his 'experiments'[77] and the normal commitments and routine of a diocesan bishop - in themselves more than enough to keep a man occupied - he could still find the time and energy to continue and even extend his ecumenical work, to care for*

---

74. *Ibid.*, p. 30.

75. Bishop Nikolai's name is not included in the list of delegates who attended this meeting (see the Minutes of the Executive Committee of the Universal Council for Life and Work, Novi Sad (Yugoslavia), September 9th -12th, 1933, p. 1). So Bishop Nikolai must have visited Novi Sad privately on this occasion.

76. See *Douglas Papers*, Vol. 51, f. 184.

77. The 'experiments' included the formation of a voluntary society of 'Sussex Church Builders', in order to raise money to help to build much-needed new churches and schools, and the setting up of a centre for spiriual healing at St. Stephen's Church, Brighton (see Jasper, *George Bell*, p. 75).

refugees, to identify himself with various social problems, and to write.[78]

However George Bell's main pre-occupation during the years before the outbreak of the Second World War was the situation in the German Evangelical (Lutheran) Church. The election of Adolf Hitler as Chancellor and virtual ruler of Germany in 1933 had immediate repercussions on that Church. In July 1933 Dr Ludwig Müller was appointed Reichsbishop, with the object of bringing the Church under strict state control; in fact it was to be known as the 'German State Christian Church'. One of his first actions, in January 1934, was to introduce a 'Muzzling Order', forbidding ministers of the Evangelical Church to express any criticism of the government.[79] He also proceeded to apply the so-called 'Aryan Paragraph', promulgated by the Prussian Synod, stating that no one who was not of pure Aryan descent could work as a minister in the German State Church.[80] A considerable number of the members of this Church accepted, or at any rate did not oppose, these draconian measures; but there was resistance and opposition, sufficient to cause a split in the German Evangelical Church; the minority that opposed Reichsbishop Müller's policies came to be known as the Confessing Church.[81]

George Bell was inevitably (though probably not unwillingly) drawn into this conflict within the German Evangelical Church, because of his position as President of the Executive Council of the Universal Christian Council of the Life and Work movement. In this capacity, he had to deal with all the church leaders of all the countries which supported this movement. From the very beginning of the struggle, he set himself the difficult

---

78. *Ibid.*, p. 75.
79. *Ibid.*, p. 106.
80. *Ibid.*, p. 105.
81. *Ibid.*, p. 100.

task of firmly opposing every policy and action which in any way threatened the spiritual autonomy and freedom of action of any part of the German Church, while at the same time avoiding any measures which would involve breaking off relations with the leaders of that Church. His aim was to persuade them to change their policies, but never to compromise. In pursuit of this aim, he wrote a number of long, complicated and carefully-worded letters,[82] which must have required hours of thought and effort. An extract from a letter he wrote to Reichsbishop Müller on January 18th, 1934, will serve as an illustration:

> *I cannot conceal the grave distress and regret with which I and members of the Christian Churches abroad have followed the most recent developments. The two very points to which I called attention and about which you gave me some positive assurances[83] have been surrendered. In reply to my first point about the Aryan Paragraph, you said that the application of the Aryan Paragraph to Church officers had been cancelled. But now that cancellation has itself been cancelled. In reply to my second point, about the suppressing and silencing of opponents, you said that you would do all you could to reach a complete union of all the ecclesiastical and theological forces in the German Evangelical Church, and that the change in the spiritual ministry was closely connected with this. But now the spiritual ministry is suspended; all opposition and criticism has been prohibited; and still sterner measures of coercion are apparently projected. How, I ask, can such a state of things be harmonised with the principles of the Christian Gospel?*

---

82. George Bell's immediate reaction to the 'Muzzling Order' was a letter of protest to The Times on January 7th, 1934, for which he received a warm letter of thanks from a young German pastor then working in London, Dietrich Bonhoeffer. They soon became close friends, and remained so to the end of Bonhoeffer's life (see Jasper, *George Bell*, p. 107).

83. A reference to a previous exchange of letters. See *ibid.*, p. 105.

Forgive me, Herr Reichsbishop, if I express myself too strongly, but my feelings are strong and I should be deceiving you and failing in my duty as President of the Universal Christian Council for Life and Work if I did not declare to you that such action, and such policy, must cause universal dismay, and must, if persisted in, evoke the strongest protests from the Christian Churches abroad to which you appealed in your memorable letter of 1 September and again in your inaugural address as Reichsbishop ...[84]

It must have been discouraging that these letters produced so little effect; nor was Bell's personal situation made easier by the fact that some of his colleagues were indifferent to his views, or even opposed them; at the meeting of the Life and Work executive committee in Novi Sad, no other member of the British delegation was present at the meeting where these problems were discussed.[85]

The application of the Aryan Paragraph, against which Bell so vigorously protested, further complicated the problem of the influx of refugees seeking asylum in Britain during the thirties. The position of those 'non-Aryan Christians' (including Christian ministers) who were deprived of their livelihood in Germany because of their Jewish ancestry was particularly difficult, since as Christians they were not eligible for help from the Jewish charities and relief organisations which helped Jews who had not converted, even if they no longer practised the Jewish religion. There was in fact no separate organisation in Britain to help these people. This problem was brought to George Bell's notice by Mrs Helen Bentwich, the secretary of the German Refugees Hospitality Committee. He responded with character-istic warmth and energy; unfortunately his efforts did not meet with much success at first. However he persisted, and in 1937 he

84. Jasper, *George Bell*, pp. 107-8.
85. *Ibid.*, p. 103.

set up a Church of England Council for non-Aryan Christians, with the object of raising money to educate children and train young people in this group. He also appealed to the High Commissioners of the Commonwealth countries, in the hope of arranging to re-settle some of the non-Aryan Christians there, but without success. Gradually he was able to arouse sympathy, and secure some financial help from his fellow-Christians, notably in his own diocese; but without his unwearying personal commitment to their cause, the situation of these refugees in England would have remained very difficult, even desperate.[86]

For Bishop Nikolai also, life was increasingly difficult. He continued to be concerned about the poverty of his diocese, which he could do so little to alleviate; in a letter to Canon Douglas, (dated May 6th, 1928), he asked Douglas if he could arrange for the Faith Press to sell some remaining copies of a book he had written in England during the war on the Serbian Orthodox Church. (The book had originally been published by John Murray.)

> *There are about 200 copies left,*' he wrote. '*Would you - or better to say, the Faith Press - take these copies at the price you like to put to it. I should like to give the obtained money to the Clerical Fund for my poor priests of the diocese.*[87]

He also felt keenly his isolation from both his English friends, and also his colleagues in the Serbian Orthodox Church. In another letter to Douglas, probably written towards the end of 1934,[88] he says:

---

86. *Ibid.*, pp. 135-146.

87. *Douglas Papers,* Vol. 51, ff. 199-200.

88. The date of the year is indecipherable but, from the reference to Bishop Irinej, it is reasonable to assume that it was 1934.

I write to wish you a right happy New Year. Though I am a little fachée [sic] with you, because you did not come, as you wrote last September. And it was most important that you did it. We had so much to ask you to inform us, specially on two questions: the birth control, and the darwinistic allegiance of some of your bishops, if it is true.

The informations of our delegate, Bishop Irineus, were very scarce. Probably it was not his fault. He was absorbed with questions of propaganda.[89]

Bishop Nikolai was also inevitably drawn into the troubled political situation in Yugoslavia during these years. Almost from the outset, the stability of the new state had suffered as a result of tension between the Serbs and the Croats, its two main ethnic components. The Croats, who had enjoyed a limited measure of autonomy in the Habsburg Empire, not unnaturally resented the more centralised system of government in the new state, centred on Belgrade. An important and intractable element in this tension was the religious difference, the Croats being predominantly Roman Catholic, and the Serbs Orthodox; in both communities religious allegiance was an important component in the sense of national and cultural identity. As early as 1922, King Alexander had set in motion negotiations for a Concordat with the Vatican which would regulate the position of Roman Catholics within his kingdom, and, he hoped, bind them more closely to the monarchy. But nothing substantial had been accomplished before King Alexander was assassinated in Marseilles in 1934.[90] However, negotiations were eventually resumed by Prince Paul, a cousin of Alexander, who headed the Council of Regency which governed the country after Alexander's death;[91] and on July 25th, 1935, a

---

89. This is probably a reference to the Life and Work conference in Fanö in Denmark, which Bishop Irinej of Novi Sad attended; he is easily recognisable in the photograph of the delegates facing p. 116 in Jasper's biography of George Bell.

90. King Alexander was assassinated by a Macedonian terrorist, acting as an agent of Croatian Ustaše emigrés, based in Italy.

draft text of a Concordat was initialled in Rome (presumably indicating provisional acceptance of its content).[92] However, further progress was impeded by the vehemently-expressed opposition of the hierarchy of the Serbian Orthodox Church. In November 1936, after a meeting of the Episcopal synod, Patriarch Varnava (Rosić) sent a formal protest to the government, and forbade Serbian deputies to vote for the Concordat when it came up for discussion in the Skupština (the lower house of the Yugoslav parliament). This happened in July, 1937.[93] It was unfortunate, perhaps, that this debate, which inevitably proved to be very stormy, coincided with the serious illness of Patriarch Varnava, who in fact died on July 23rd, 1937. A special service to pray for the Patriarch's recovery had been arranged in the Serbian Orthodox Cathedral in Belgrade, to be followed by a procession through the adjoining streets. Because of the tense political situation, the government forbade all public demonstrations and processions at this time. However the crowds assembled outside the cathedral took no notice of this order; as a result there were violent clashes between the crowds and the police, during which two bishops were injured. These events were reported in some details in the British Press.[94] A report from the Belgrade correspondent of the *Daily Telegraph* concluded with the words:

'The capital (Belgrade) is in a state of ferment this evening (July 20th). It is believed that after today's scenes ... there is no possibility that M. Stoyadinovitch[95] will succeed in pushing

---

91. A Regency was necessary because Alexander's heir, King Peter, was still a minor. Until his father's death, he was at school in England.

92. For a summary of the terms of the Concordat and the circumstances leading up to it, see Stella Alexander, *The Triple Myth*, pp. 28-34.

93. *Ibid.*, p. 34.

94. See the *Douglas Papers*, Vol. 51, f. 95: an article in the Daily Telegraph for July 22nd by William Teeling, entitled *Serbian Church's Challenge to Prince Paul, over Vatican Concordat.*

95. Milan Stojadinović, Prime Minister of Yugoslavia from 1935 to 1939.

through the ratification of the Concordat by the end of July, as intended.'[96]

This forecast proved to be correct. The text of the Concordat was not sent to the Senate (the upper house of the Yugoslav Parliament) for ratification; and on December 12th, 1937 it was announced that there would be no further proposals for a Concordat between Yugoslavia and the Vatican. As part of its strategy of opposition to the Concordat, the Serbian Orthodox hierarchy sent Bishop Irinej of Dalmatia to England in the hope of enlisting the support of the Anglican Church.[97] Bishop Nikolai, presumably with the same intention, sent to the *Church Times* an English translation of an open letter which he had written to Mgr Korozhez (Anton Korošec), a Slovene Roman Catholic who was then Minister of the Interior in the Yugoslav government. This letter was a lengthy and strongly-worded protest against the ill-treatment of Orthodox Serbs (official and unofficial) by Roman Catholics during the period when the Concordat was still under discussion. It was published in the *Church Times,* slightly abbreviated, on September 3rd, 1937. It is clear from the occasional use of foreign syntax and turns of phrase that Bishop Nikolai had made this translation himself; however it is not clear whether he was acting independently in submitting it to the *Church Times,* or whether he was acting on behalf of the Serbian Orthodox hierarchy.

The letter begins with an opening paragraph written in some-what bombastic language, unlike Bishop Nikolai's usual style, at any rate when he writes in English:

Sir - In an age when the bloody Caesars persecuted Christians by fire and sword, the apologist-confessors of our

---

96. *Douglas Papers,* Vol. 51, f. 94.

97. *Ibid.,* f. 93. Bishop Irinej of Dalmatia was one of the Serbian ordinands who had completed his theological studies in Oxford during the First World War.

*glorious religion wrote to those Caesars, proving objectively
and with dignity, that danger threatened the Roman Empire
not from Christians but from the pagans. Persecutions under-
taken by you through your agents in recent weeks against the
Orthodox Church, in would-be defence of the State, have
imposed on me the honourable task to appear before you as
Bishop of the pursued Church, as her Apologist.*

*The difference between the former and the present circum-
stances is very great. The Roman Empire was constituted on
pagan idolatry religion, and Caesars persecuted Christendom
as something new and unknown, something that was reported
as dangerous to the State. Our State, however, has been born
by the very spirit and truth of our Orthodox independent and
national Church,[98] which fact cannot be unknown to you.
And you have launched the persecution of the mother so as
to protect the daughter.[99] The whole world is staggered by
your invention that the daughter is menaced by her own
mother, and before your super-zeal in protecting the daughter
from her parent.[100]*

Bishop Nikolai then goes on to describe the various injuries
and injustices suffered by the Orthodox Serbs at the hands of the
police and agents of the Ministry of the Interior: the attacks on
the crowd outside the Orthodox Cathedral in Belgrade, 'when
they beat up the barehanded people, members of Parliament,
bishops and priests assembled for universal prayer; when they
tore up church banners, smashed crosses and ripped priests'
vestments ...' He also complained about the dismissal of 'minor
officials' who had dared to utter any criticism of the Concordat,

---

98. Bishop Nikolai is not quite accurate here, unless by the word 'state' he means
the former kingdom of Serbia. The kingdom of Yugoslavia was in fact multi-
confessional, with a large Roman Catholic population, as well as a considerable
number of Moslems.

99. The mother-daughter imagery refers to the Orthodox belief that it was the
Western Church that was responsible for the Schism of 1054, which split the
Christian Church.

100. *Douglas Papers*, Vol. 51, f. 202.

the strict surveillance of Orthodox clergy; and the tearing down of black mourning flags from both public buildings and private houses after the death of Patriarch Varnava. There is also a passage which throws an interesting and revealing light on the way in which these punitive acts were carried out:

> *It is very fortunate under the circumstances that the majority of the police officials are men of the people themselves, that is conscientious and patriotic, who, feeling the storm of national anger against the Great Injustice,*[101] *whose name you have indexed, refrain from persecuting St. Sava's Church.* '[102]

Towards the end of this long letter, there is an interesting reminder that Bishop Nikolai, for all his unusual gifts as a writer and a theologian, had not forgotten that he was a man of the people:

> *But my soul aches,* he writes, *because such tortures fall on small officials, peasants, artisans and priests who are family men, although I know that God will reward them a hundred-fold and gild their wounds. I appeal to you for them. Leave them in peace. You can strike us Orthodox Bishops, if you find that we are guilty. Strike even if we are innocent, but spare them ...*[103]

The response to these appeals in England was probably rather disappointing to Bishop Nikolai and his fellow Serbs. The editor of the *Church Times* introduced Bishop Nikolai's open letter in distinctly non-commital language, describing it as 'an outspoken document ... concerning the Concordat with Rome, and the resultant persecution of Orthodox Christians.'[104] Harold

---

101. Bishop Nikolai's name for the Concordat in this open letter.

102. The Serbian Orthodox Church is often described as the 'Church of St Sava', since it was St Sava who secured its autocephalous status in the thirteenth century.

103. *Douglas Papers,* Vol. 51, f. 202.

104. *Ibid.*

Temperley, certainly a fervent admirer of the Serbs,[105] had already written a letter to *The Times* (dated July 29th, 1937), supporting Prince Paul's ecclesiastical policy, and expressing regret at the opposition of the Serbian Orthodox hierarchy to the Concordat, which he attributed to memories of the schism of 1054. 'In England,' he concluded, 'we should look rather to the results of a tolerant and statesmanlike action than to the temporary ebullitions of resentment which it is bound to excite. Tolerance is a plant of slow growth in the Near East, and we should welcome and cherish its appearance.'[106]

More significant, perhaps, because of its ecclesiastical provenance, is a memorandum (marked 'private') written by Harold Buxton, Bishop of Gibraltar, subsequent to the withdrawal of the Concordat in October 1937. After reporting on his conversation with various individuals concerned in these events, he wrote:

> *I am decidedly of the opinion that the Orthodox would be wise to drop their agitation for 'satisfaction', which only means further humiliation for the Prime Minister [Stoyadinovitch] and would inevitably involve the Orthodox Church with the political opposition; it might lead to civil war. On many grounds ... it seems undesirable that the Church should attach itself in close fashion to any one party or group of parties ... Therefore I have intimated to Metropolitan Dosithei [107] that (in my view), while we of the Anglican Church have whole-heartedly supported them up to this moment, he must not count upon our support in further public agitation, now that the Concordat has been withdrawn.'*

---

105. His history of Serbia, written in 1917, while Serbia was still under enemy occupation, is still a valuable guide to the history of the Serbs up to that date.

106. *Douglas Papers*, Vol. 51, f. 96.

107. The Orthodox Metropolitan of Zagreb. He died in Belgrade in 1945, after suffering persecution by the Ustaše government of Croatia.

If the Concordat were to be re-introduced in its present form, then we would of course again throw our weight on the Orthodox side. [108]

The strong feelings expressed in Bishop Nikolai's open letter to the *Church Times* might at first seem surprising, in view of his enduring affection and respect for the Old Catholics, at whose theological faculty in Berne he had studied.[109] However, it should be borne in mind that he was protesting primarily against illegal acts of violence committed in the name of the Concordat, not - at any rate openly - against the principle behind it. These acts had in fact been fully reported in the British Press, but possibly he was not aware of this. Also, in Yugoslavia at that time (and subsequently) religious differences, especially between Roman Catholics and Orthodox, had strong political overtones - similar to those between Catholics and Protestants in Northern Ireland. It was the power of Rome that the Orthodox feared, not the western form of Christianity. As regards Bishop Nikolai's personal feelings, there is nothing in either his writings or his personal relationships to indicate that he felt any hostility towards the religious views of other confessions.

In 1936, Bishop Nikolai once more became Bishop of Žiča. However, he continued to visit his former diocese; and there is an interesting picture of him, on one of these visits, in Rebecca West's well-known book, *Black Lamb and Grey Falcon*. It seems that Bishop Nikolai visited Ochrid to celebrate the Orthodox Easter there in 1937, at the same time as Rebecca West was also visiting Ochrid, as part of her travels through Macedonia. She was anxious to see Bishop Nikolai, and talk to him if possible; and she was finally able to do so during an informal outdoor lunch, after the celebration of the Easter Liturgy:

---

108. *Douglas Papers*, Vol. 51, ff. 101-2.
109. See below, p. 74.

Bishop Nikolai of Ochrid in 1928

The Church of the Holy Wisdom (St Sofija), Ochrid

He struck me now, she wrote, *as when I had seen him for the first time the previous year, as the most remarkable human being I have ever met, not because he was wise or good, for I still have no idea to what degree he is either, but because he was the supreme magician. He had command over the means of making magic, in his great personal beauty, which was of the lion's kind, and in the thundering murmur of his voice, which by its double quality, grand, yet guttural, suggests that he could speak to gods and men and beasts. He had full knowledge of what comfort men seek in magic, and how they long to learn that defeat is not defeat and that love is serviceable.* [110]

At the end of the *al fresco* lunch (consisting of cold lamb, hard-boiled eggs, sheep's cheese, cold fried fish, unleavened bread and young garlic) the members of the company cracked their hard-boiled eggs together.

He (Bishop Nikolai) gave me a hard-boiled egg, and took one himself, and made me strike his at the same time. 'The one that cracks the other's egg will be the master,' he said. [111]

Just before the party broke up, she continues:

Then he made a civil reference to my husband and myself, expressing pleasure that people should come all the way from England to Ochrid: and I found the pale old abbot of Sveti

110. *Black Lamb and, Grey Falcon* (Paperback edition, 1982), p. 720. Bishop Nikolai and his Anglican friends would hardly have accepted the term 'magic' as a description of the Liturgy of the Orthodox Church; but this account does convey the charismatic aspect of his personality, of which many people were aware.

111. *Ibid.*, p. 721.

Naum[112] standing by me, like a courteous ghost, holding out an egg in his thin hand. 'He says,' translated the Bishop, whose English is beautiful, as befits one who once preached in St Paul's Cathedral 'that he is giving you this egg to take to your parish priest, as a symbol that the Anglican Church and the Orthodox Church are united in the risen Christ, not the buried Christ but the Christ who lives for ever. Have you got a parish priest?' he enquired very doubtfully. I said, truthfully, but perhaps evasively, 'I will take it to my cousin, who is priest of a church that was built when the Anglican and the Orthodox Church were one,' and tied up the egg in my handkerchief.[113]

No doubt Bishop Nikolai was satisfied by her reply, and happy to think that an Anglican priest would receive this gift from Ochrid, and appreciate its significance.

By the autumn of 1939, Britain was already at war with Germany, and Yugoslavia was facing an uncertain future, in spite of Prince Paul's attempts to keep on good terms with the Nazi government. Bishop Nikolai's sad and anxious thoughts at that time are reflected in a short and poignant letter to Canon Douglas, written at the end of 1939:

Episkop Žički [no exact date]

My dear Canon Douglas,
  I am writing to wish you a right happy Christmas. The darker is the time which we are going through the brighter shines the light of our great and wonderful Lord and Saviour.

---

112.   An ancient Orthodox monastery, on the southern shore of Lake Ochrid.
113.   *Black Lamb and Grey Falcon,* pp. 723-4.

May His light shine in your home and in your dear and suffering motherland.

The Word of God, which the English dispersed all over the world, shall save England. This is my faith, and also my prayer, to Jesus Christ our Saviour.

With best regards,
                    Yours very truly,
                    + Bishop Nikolai. [114]

---

114. *Douglas Papers,* Vol. 51, f. 203.

III: THE SECOND WORLD WAR (1939 - 1945)

Throughout the duration of the Second World War, George Bell and Nikolai Velimirović were completely out of touch. It is true that, until the occupation of Yugoslavia by the Axis powers in 1941, some contact was maintained between the Church of England and the Serbian Orthodox Church,[1] but there was no personal contact between the two bishops. For both of them, though in different ways, the war was a time of testing; it was even a traumatic experience, which affected both the outward circumstances of their lives and also their spiritual journey.

Materially, George Bell fared better, since Britain was never under enemy occupation (if it had been, that would probably have been the end of George Bell).[2] Shortly after the outbreak of the war, he and Mrs Bell left the Episcopal residence at Farnham Palace, and lived (no doubt in reasonable comfort) in Brighton; the Palace was put at the disposal of the education authority and used to accommodate school-children evacuated from London. In 1942 they returned to Chichester, though they only used half of the palace. The routine work of administering the diocese had to be carried on as normally as possible, in spite of the difficulties caused by food and petrol rationing, black-out, and reduced man-power as clergy left to become army chaplains. Moreover George Bell willingly undertook an increased load of pastoral work, ministering to refugees, and sometimes entertaining them in the palace; and also caring for service personnel, (especially after the south of England became a military zone), and keeping in touch with those of his own diocesan clergy who were on war service.[3] Nevertheless the basic pattern of his peace-time life and

---

1. See below, p. 57ff.
2. During the years immediately before the outbreak of the war, George Bell was clearly *persona non grata* in Germany (see Jasper, *George Bell,* p. 142).
3. *Ibid.,* pp. 86-91.

activities was maintained; and he and his wife suffered no more hardship or danger than the majority of civilians in wartime England.

George Bell's warfare was in another sphere; and the key to it can be found in some words addressed to the clergy of his diocese immediately after the outbreak of the war:

The Church, he said, *was charged with the Gospel of God's redeeming love, and its function was to bear witness to the moral law which was both supra-national and super-natural; and it should not remain silent when law and justice were at stake.*[4]

For Bell himself, this meant the unremitting pursuit, throughout the war, of certain specific objectives: opposition to military measures which deliberately damaged civilians, and in particular the 'saturation bombing' of German cities; continually stressing, in speech and writing, the distinction between the Nazi government in Germany, which he regarded as something evil which should be destroyed, and the people of Germany; and maintaining contact with Churches in enemy territory or under enemy occupation. He also believed in supporting overtures for a negotiated peace, under suitable conditions.

His views on the need to distinguish between Hitler's government and the German people are clearly summarised in his book *Christianity and World Order:*

Germany and National Socialism are not the same thing. The West can never make terms with the National Socialist ideology. But the West can make terms with Germany, if only

---

4. Ibid., p. 86.

Germany could go through a revolution such as Britain and France have gone through.[5]

The following quotation from Jasper's biography of George Bell is a typical statement on the subject of saturation bombing:

It is barbarous to make unarmed women and children the object of attack ... If Europe is civilised at all, what can excuse the bombing of towns by night, and the terrorising of non-combatants who work by day and cannot sleep when darkness comes? ... Is it not possible for the British government to make a solemn declaration that they for their part will refrain from night bombing ... provided that the German Government will give the same declaration?[6]

His main forum was the House of Lords, where he had sat since July, 1938. Here he took every possible opportunity to oppose the so-called 'Vansittartism',[7] (which refused to distinguish between National Socialism and the German people), to condemn the bombing of civilians, and to urge that a minimum supply of food-stuffs should be available for the occupied countries. 'His tenacity of purpose and his fearlessness in the face of opposition and criticism were revealed in the House of Lords as nowhere else,' wrote his biographer.[8]

George Bell paid a price for expressing his view so forcibly. He had some supporters, including the military historian Liddell Hart; but he also incurred considerable unpopularity, and had no

---

5.   George Bell, *Christianity and World Order*, pp. 105-6 (quoted in Jasper, *George Bell*, p. 260).

6.   *Ibid.*, p. 262.

7.   'Vansittartism': derived from the name of Sir Robert Vansittart, chief diplomatic adviser to the government, and author of a book entitled *Black Record*, in which he argued that the Germans as a nation had always been warlike and arrogant, and would continue to be so.

8.   Jasper, *George Bell*, p. 256.

observable success in influencing government policies. In a BBC broadcast shortly after his death, the speaker made the following comment on his impact on the House of Lords:

> *There was no one whose speeches were followed with a closer, or at times, more painful attention, when he raised, as he almost invariably did, a moral issue. That is not to say that he was a popular speaker; there were quite a number of excellent peers who couldn't take his speeches at all. They found them so acutely irritating that they could hardly bear to listen in silence. It is difficult to say why those who differed from so saintly a man found him so tremendously irritating, and so acutely provocative in public, although for the most part they had an enormous admiration for him in his private life.*[9]

It is generally thought that it was the unpopularity resulting from his wartime speeches that prevented him from receiving the ecclesiastical promotion which his considerable talents would otherwise have warranted. He was the obvious successor to William Temple as Archbishop of Canterbury in 1944; but he was passed over in favour of Geoffrey Fisher.[10]

In describing George Bell's wartime activities, his biographer comments on the weakness, as he sees it, of his intellectual position:

> *Fundamentally he believed that war was wrong,* he writes. *Yet he refused to become a pacifist, and continued to maintain that Great Britain went to war for a just cause - for freedom and justice against violence and brute force. He failed to see clearly that even a war for a just cause must be - on his own admission - destructive, wasteful of life and resources, and*

---

9. Extract from a broadcast talk by Lord Longford, (then Lord Pakenham), on February 25th, 1959, quoted in Jasper, *George Bell*, p. 286.
10. Jasper, *George Bell*, pp. 284-6; see also Owen Chadwick, *Michael Ramsey: a Life*, pp. 87-8.

poisonous. As the struggle dragged on, he deplored the retreat from the original high ideals; yet war itself made such a retreat inevitable.' [11]

It could be argued that this was the very fact that George Bell could not accept; not on intellectual grounds, but because of his prophetic insight into the moral issues involved. It was under wartime conditions, it would seem, that he became aware of this prophetic insight within himself; and it is a tribute to his courage and his integrity that he never attempted to stifle it.[12]

Prince Paul, the head of the Regency Council which governed Yugoslavia during the minority of King Peter II, hoped to be able to keep his country neutral when the war between Germany and Britain, France and Poland broke out in September 1939. Until April, 1941, he succeeded. Up to that time, contacts were maintained between the Church of England and the Serbian Orthodox Church. On the Anglican side, the most active participants were Canon J. A. Douglas, and Harold Buxton, Bishop of Gibraltar, whose area of jurisdiction included south-east Europe. As George Bell was not involved, these contacts have no direct relevance to the relationship between him and Bishop Nikolai; but they are of interest for the light they throw on the connection between the two Churches, and also on Bishop Nikolai's personal situation in his own country at that time.

Shortly after the war broke out, the Bishop of Gibraltar, who was then travelling through south-east Europe, wrote to Canon Douglas,[13] enclosing a hand-written list of suggestions:

---

11. Jasper, *George Bell*, p. 283.
12. Frank Field, in a lecture given to the Friends of Lambeth Palace Library in 1996, stresses the moral consistency of George Bell's views during the Second World War, though he expresses some doubt as to whether Bell was conscious of this as 'an act of prophecy' (see *Lambeth Palace Library Annual Review*, 1996, pp. 60-61).
13. This letter is dated October 22nd, 1939, and written from the Hotel Esplanade in Zagreb.

Could the F. R. Council, or another body, send our Church papers weekly to a selected list of friends (Sitters[14] would distribute)?

Another suggestion I wish to make is that we (the F. R.C. ?)[15] invite both +Nicholai Velimirović and +Irinei of Novi Sad for a month's visit to England. Such an invitation would make a great impression out here. Irinei of Novi Sad is intimate with Gavrilo,[16] while +Nicholai is at present isolated from the H[oly] Synod and is not on good terms with the Patriarch. An invitation to both men would help to restore unity between the 2 groups.

A similar invitation to Stephan of Sofia.

A 'decoration' or a Cross from the Archbishop of Cant. for all three men.'[17]

On January 6th 1940, the BBC broadcast a message of greeting composed by Canon Douglas, on the occasion of the Orthodox Christmas (celebrated on January 7th).[18] Later that year, towards the end of April, an Anglican delegation consisting of Canon Douglas, Harold Buxton (Bishop of Gibraltar), and Dr Headlam (Bishop of Gloucester) set out on a visit to south-east Europe, visiting first Romania, then Yugoslavia and Bulgaria. They spent Easter in Bucharest, and then went to Yugoslavia in time to present the official greetings of the Church of England to Patriarch Gavrilo on May 5th, the eve of St George's Day in the Orthodox Calendar. After this they visited the mausoleum of the Karađorđević dynasty at Oplenac in central Serbia. Just before they visited Patriarch Gavrilo (who was then in Sremski Karlovci, near Novi Sad), they spent a short time in Belgrade,

---

14. Anglican chaplain in Belgrade.
15. The Church of England Council for Foreign Relations.
16. Gavrilo Dožić, elected Patriarch of the Serbian Orthodox Church in 1938, in succession to Patriarch Varnava.
17. *Douglas Papers,* Vol. 51, f. 112. There is no evidence that these suggestions were carried out.
18. *Ibid.,* ff. 117-18.

where they had a lengthy interview with a journalist on the staff of the newspaper *Politika*. In the course of this interview the journalist (Siniša Paunović) asked them which other Orthodox church dignitaries they knew in Yugoslavia, apart from Patriarch Gavrilo. The Bishop of Gibraltar replied:

'Dositej (Vasić), the Metropolitan of Zagreb, Dr Irinej (Djordjević), the Bishop of Šibenik, Rev. Djordjević, the Bishop of Bačka,[19] *Dr Jovan, Bishop of Niš, and, needless to stress, Dr Nikolai Velimirović, the Bishop of Žiča.*

'At the mentioning of the name of Dr Nikolai, the Bishop of Žiča, the face of Bishop Buckston[20] becomes unusually delighted and enthusiastic, and forgetting for the moment his laconic way of answering questions, he adds:

I know Dr Nikolai from the times of the war, when he used to speak in St Paul's Cathedral, where ten or even twenty thousand English people used to listen to him. You cannot imagine it. I was present in my own person so many times in the Church when Dr Nikolai was speaking ...

'As if afraid lest Bishop Buckston would omit to say everything of the great friend of England, Dr. Nikolai, Prof. Douglas[21] continues:

Even today, Bishop Nikolai calls me Brother Douglas. I was one of the committee that welcomed Dr Nikolai on his first visit to London.[22] *Personally I highly esteem Dr Nikolai as an ecclesiastical man, and I like him very much indeed. I*

---

19. The Bishop of Gibraltar is not accurate at this point; the Bishop of Bačka was Irinej Ćirić.
20. The Bishop of Gibraltar's name is spelt in this way because there is no letter 'x' in the Cyrillic alphabet used in Serbia.
21. Canon Douglas was Chairman of Convocation in the University of London.
22. Fr Nikolai Velimirović first paid a short visit to England in 1910.

was told that Dr Nikolai's character was regarded as peculiar,[23] but I do not understand that ... Even today people in England and especially London, ask where Dr Nikolai is. He was the first non-Anglican to be allowed to speak in St Paul's Cathedral. Even now, if he would come, all London would rush to hear him.[24]

On May 5th the delegation visited Patriarch Gavrilo at his summer residence in Sremski Karlovci, near Novi Sad. There they were entertained at an official dinner, also attended by the British Ambassador to Yugoslavia. In proposing a toast, the Patriarch spoke warmly about the relationship between the Anglican Church and the Serbian Orthodox Church:

With particularly deep satisfaction, he said, I want to point out the traditional bonds between the Church of England and the Orthodox Church, linking the two for centuries with mutual Christian love, evangelic [sic] sincerity and fraternal collaboration.[25]

The next day the Anglican party travelled south to Oplenac. This was just north of Bishop Nikolai's diocese, and he came there to greet them. The meeting was reported (as was the interview in Belgrade) in *Politika:*

The meeting between the Anglican clergymen and the Bishop of Žiča was unusually touching and cordial. Professor Douglas[26] exclaimed in Serbian: 'God bless our

---

23. The words used in the original Serbo-Croatian report in *Politika* at this point are *raznovrstan značaj;* 'regarded with mixed feelings' would be a better rendering in English.

24. *Douglas Papers,* Vol. 51, f. 138. The interview seems to have been conducted in a mixture of languages; the text quoted here is the English translation of the Serbian article, probably made by the journalist. Though somewhat foreign in style, it is substantially accurate. The original Serbo-Croatian text is affixed to f. 139.

25. *Douglas Papers,* Vol. 51, f. 140.

26. Canon Douglas is given this title because of his connection with London University.

brother, Bishop Nikolai!' and Bishop Nikolai thanked him
heartily for these cordial greetings.

Bishop Nikolai then celebrated a requiem at the tomb of
King Alexander, where the Anglican visitors left a wreath. There
was a lunch at a nearby hotel, when various speeches were made,
and an actor from one of the leading Belgrade theatres recited
Psalm 39. The newspaper report concluded:

> *On parting with Bishop Nikolai and his suite, Professor*
> *Douglas exclaimed to the assembled visitors:* 'Long live the
> Serbian Patriarch! Long live Bishop Nikolai!' [27]

The other Anglican clergymen joined in the cheers of Canon
Douglas; then they said good-bye to Bishop Nikolai, and
returned to Belgrade.[28]

It was destined to be a very long 'good-bye'. Soon after the
Anglican delegation returned home, the period of quiescent,
'phony' war in the West ended. After the fall of France and the
Battle of Britain, with most of western Europe under enemy
occupation, travel to south-east Europe became virtually impossible.
Meanwhile the situation in Yugoslavia was becoming increasingly
tense. In the spring of 1941, Prince Paul signed a Tripartite Pact
with the Axis powers, pledging the future support of Yugoslavia.
This provoked a storm of popular indignation, expressed in the
slogan 'Better War than the Pact'.[29] Patriarch Gavrilo paid a personal
visit to Prince Paul to protest against the Pact, at which he said
that he had the support of all his bishops, and particularly that of
Bishop Irinej of Dalmatia and Bishop Nikolai of Žiča.[30] The

---

27. *Douglas Papers,* Vol. 51, f. 144; taken from the English translation of a newspaper
report in *Politika* for May 7th, 1940.

28. *Douglas Papers,* Vol. 51, f. 145.

29. The assonance of the original words of the slogan: *bolje rat nego pakt,* is unfortunately
lost in translation.

30. Đoka Slijepčević, *Istorija Srpske pravoslavne crkve,* III, pp. 37-40.

opposition culminated in a *putsch* carried out the night of March 26th-27th, when King Peter (then aged 17) was declared to be officially of age, and Prince Paul was deposed. Indignation was succeeded by a mood of euphoria, induced by the feeling that the nation had recovered its freedom of action and restored its national honour. Patriarch Gavrilo's rôle in these events was commented on favourably in England, in an article in *The Times*:

> *During the crisis which has shaken the Yugoslav nation, the part played by Gavrilo, Patriarch of the Serbian Orthodox Church, is reminiscent of the English bishops in the Middle Ages, when the Church determined the policy of Kings and was the keeper of their conscience. Although the full history of his involvement in this fatal week is not known, the Yugoslav people instinctively feel that if he had not resisted the Regent, and mobilised all the forces of the Serbian Orthodox Church for this purpose, Yugoslavia would right up to this day have been one of Hitler's vassal states.*[31]

But the euphoria proved to be short-lived, and German retribution came swiftly. It began with a massive aerial bombardment on April 6th, 1941, quickly followed by a military invasion. Yugoslav resistance soon collapsed, and on April 17th the army capitulated. The long period of wartime occupation and subjection had begun.

Serbia was placed under direct military occupation. There was also a Serbian civilian administration (under the military governor), headed by General Nedić, a former minister of war. Bishop Nikolai, as a well-known Anglophile, and a firm supporter of Patriarch Gavrilo's opposition to the Tripartite Pact, was interned in the convent at Ljubostinja,[32] not far from Žiča.

.31. *Ibid.,* pp. 47-8.

32. Ljubostinja was a medieval royal foundation, founded in 1395 by Princess Milica, the widow of Prince Lazar who had been killed in the Battle of Kosovo in 1389. Later she became a nun in the convent. See Anne Kindersley, *The Mountains of Serbia,* pp. 140-143.

Patriarch Gavrilo was also interned, in Rakovica Monastery. Later, in the spring of 1944, they were both removed to another monastery, at Vojlovac, near Pančevo. After a short stay there they were visited by General Nedić, in August, 1944. Soon after this, they were told to make preparations for departure, and were taken, first by road, then by train, to Budapest. From there they were taken in a goods train to Dachau concentration camp. Patriarch Gavrilo described their experience in his *Memoirs:*

> *We were so exhausted from the journey that we were no good for anything. But the Germans took no notice of this, and after our arrival they packed us into the infamous barracks where life was impossible.*[33]

In fact they did not have to endure the worst horrors of the concentration camp. They were kept separate from the other prisoners, in a so-called 'honourable bunker', allowed to wear their own clothes, and not forced to go out to work. But their movements were confined to the bunker, and a very small court-yard surrounded by high walls. Nor did their incarceration last very long. In the spring of 1945, before Dachau was liberated by the Americans (on May 8th), they were released, as a result of the intervention of Hermann Neubacher, the German envoy plenipotentiary to Serbia, and sent, first to Bavaria, and then to Vienna;[34] finally they made contact with some representatives of the Nedić Serbian administration and went with them to Kitzbühel. Here they were received, not very cordially, by the American army authorities.[35] From then on, the movements of

---

33. Slijepčević, *Istorija Srpske pravoslavne crkve,* III, p. 66.

34. This visit to Vienna is confirmed in the account of Bishop Nikolai's conversation with George Bell in November, 1945, recorded in George Bell's diary (see below, p. 66).

35. Slijepčević, *Istorija Srpske pravoslavne crkve,* III, pp. 66-74. For part of this account, Slijepčević relies on the *Memoirs* of the German plenipotentiary Hermann Neubacher (see *ibid,* p. 74, note 42). His other main source, the *Memoirs* of Patriarch Gavrilo, is silent on the period from his arrival in Dachau until its liberation by the Americans on May 8th, 1945.

both men are rather difficult to follow.[36] Bishop Nikolai managed to make his way to Salzburg, in the company of some escaped Yugoslav prisoners of war, and eventually came to London, where he had been invited to take part in the christening of the exiled King Peter's son, the Crown Prince Alexander. It was on this occasion that Bishop Nikolai once more met George Bell, after an interval of over twelve years.

Patriarch Gavrilo had also been invited to the christening of the Crown Prince. Before coming to London, he made a short visit to Rome. He was unable to stay long in London, as the British government refused to extend his visitor's visa. After leaving London, he spent a short time in Czechoslovakia, at the invitation of the President, Eduard Beneš. Eventually he returned to Belgrade, broken in health, in November 1945.[37]

---

36. Before leaving Yugoslavia, Bishop Nikolai and Patriarch Gavrilo visited Slovenia, where remnants of the royalist Yugoslav army were fighting a rear-guard action against Tito's Partisans.

37. Slijepčević, *Istorija Srpske pravoslavne crkve*, III, pp. 82-3.

IV: THE POST - WAR YEARS

The circumstances of Bishop Nikolai's arrival in England in the autumn of 1945 were very different from those of his previous visit in November 1927.

> *After the war,* wrote Stephen Graham, *he was brought to an England which barely remembered him. He was at Westminster Abbey at the baptism of King Peter's son and heir, the little Alexander. He preached a very moving sermon at the Serb chapel in the house in Egerton Gardens. But there was no place for him in England as there had been during the First World War.*[1]

It was not only the lapse of time which affected Bishop Nikolai's position; there were also political reasons. During the war, from 1943 onwards, Britain had supported the communist-dominated Partisans, who were now in control of Yugoslavia; meanwhile Bishop Nikolai had maintained contacts with the official wartime administration of Serbia,[2] now discredited; and he was visiting England at the invitation of the exiled royalist government of Yugoslavia, soon to be repudiated. So it was interesting, and indeed significant, that one of the first events of this post-war visit was a reunion between Bishop Nikolai and George Bell, a meeting which is described in some detail in Bell's *Diary*.[3]

---

1. See Stephen Graham's short biographical account of Bishop Nikolai, written immediately after his death in 1954 (*Bell Papers,* Vol 59, f. 157).

2. See above, p. 63.

3. George Bell's *Diary* was not kept very systematically; there are considerable gaps, interspersed with detailed entries on specific occasions. One of these was a series of entries in 1945 when he recorded conversations with people from whom he had been cut off during the war, including Pastor Niemöller and Bishop Nikolai. From the context of the entry relating to Bishop Nikolai, it appears that the meeting with him took place in London.

This entry,[4] written partly in note form, is headed: Bishop
Nikolai Velimirović, and runs as follows:

*Talk at 24 Windsor Court, Moscow Road W2, 16 Nov.
1945. He had come with Patriarch Gavrilo to christen King
Peter's son. I had not seen him since 1933 in Novi Sad. He
had changed greatly. He was worn, rather spare, beard more
grey than black - and clearly suffering. His body he said was
weak but his spirit well. He was sad - with all that his country
had endured, and his own 4 years in concentration camp[5] -
partly at Dachau with Gavrilo (despatched Gestapo) and
Niemöller (whom he saw but never spoke to). He was taken
from Dachau to Vienna, to a Gestapo Hotel.[6] Negić [Nedić],
Serb Prime Minister, asked Gavrilo and Nicholai to join him
in government and pushed him (I think 3 times).[7] But they
refused - their flock was in the forest with Mihailović, another
part with Tito and they could not rule over a 1/3rd. N. and G.
were asked to form a government, but they refused - they
were trained for other work than government. I asked him
about Mihailović[8] - had I been right about praising him (he
knew my sermon) in 1941?[9] Yes, he said, nothing to take
away: praise him now, and fully - a good man, a religious
man, with purity about him - he wants a constitutional
monarchy. But Tito (whom Churchill boasted of himself
discovering in a speech of 1944) is a 'Satanic man', like
Lenin. Stalin is even worse: his régime terrible. Yugoslavia is*

---

4. *Bell Papers*, Vol. 258, ff. 128-9. This entry is written in very small cramped,
    handwriting, almost impossible to read in places.
5. This is not quite accurate; during most of Bishop Nikolai's wartime internment
    he was under house-arrest in Yugoslavia, and spent only a few months in
    Dachau concentration camp (see above, p. 63).
6. Cf. Slijepčević, *Istorija*, III, p. 68.
7. I have found no independent proof of this.
8. For a detailed account of the wartime resistance movement in Yugoslavia led
    by General Draža Mihailović, see Michael Lees, *The Rape of Serbia* (1990).
    There were also Serbs among Tito's Partisans.
9.   I have not so far been able to trace this sermon among George Bell's papers.

now like Ukraine, part of Soviet state[10] - and Bolsheviks behave to Chrns [Christians] there just as Bolsheviks behaved in 1917-18 against Chrns in Russia. Atheism. We spoke of [the] future. He quoted Matt. 21:44. It is that (who falls) on the stone shall be broken in pieces but on whomsoever it shall fall it will scatter him as dust.[11] Our Lord speaks. Jewry - a terrible judgement. Unless nations turn to God, this is what will happen to them. He was full of warning against Soviet Russia - atheistic. And against easy acceptance of the new kind of 'Panslavism' preached from Moscow, brutal atheism also from Belgrade. Christian Slavs ashamed of it. (Why should Vansittart praise Panslavism as natural - in this form?) Very different from the evangelistic Panslavism [praised] by Dostoyevski. And that this atheistic Panslavism [is] not believed by vast numbers of Slavs who are religious. Moscow dominion over 50 million Slavs is its way. But countless Slavs, in Yugoslavia, Roumania,[12] Bulgaria resist this. We simply must not abandon all Eastern Europe to Soviet[s]. There is only one point of view in the East ... It seems a simple thing, administratively. But it is not right.

Nicholai spoke of what the Churches should say to statesmen. He would like a world conference of Churches (but ... I told him of the World Council)[13] which should speak: 'We praise you for your democracy - it is good - it is founded on Christian principles - but it is not enough. You need to turn to God.' He admired [the] Christianity of British statesmen (he mentioned other State leaders: de Gaulle, a Christian), most important statesmen are Christians. Encourage them. Very

---

10. This was before Yugoslavia's break with the Comintern in 1948.

11. *And whomsoever shall fall on this stone shall be broken; but on whomsoever it shall fall, it will grind him to powder* (A.V.)

12. The Roumanians are not Slavs, but most of them are Orthodox; presumably this is why Bishop Nikolai links them with the Orthodox Slavs of Yugoslavia and Bulgaria.

13. The first formal meeting of the World Council of Churches did not take place until 1948, in Amsterdam; but preparations for it had been well advanced before the outbreak of the Second World War.

pleased that many of new Govt [are] believers.[14] Britain has certainly made mistakes, but her people will help her - how? By kind thoughts, words, especially by prayer. England the bulwark of the white people and of Christianity. If barbarians broke up Britain, it would be the end.

He spoke of God's presence with him in prison, and of angels, his real experience of God's care and love. Suffering had taught him what nothing else could have done. He had 3 requests he asked me to support, had mentioned (1) already to the Apb of C.[15] (he spoke so gratefully of Randall - [said] he was like a father to me, he took me to his heart).

Training new priests for Serbia. 3000 priests they had had. But 1000 had been killed by Germans and Russians.[16] There were many young men, and suitable, waiting to be trained - in camps in different places. Let British (and Americans) train 200 in a seminary in USA or Canada or S. Africa.[17] More than 2000 in Yugoslavia but 100 outside ...[18]

World Conference of Churches. And regular meetings of heads of Churches. Archbishop Fisher had told him of the World Council meeting in Geneva[19] - also of the Lambeth Conference.[20] All good. But Heads of State meet constantly,

---

14.   I.e. the Labour government elected in May, 1945.

15.   The Archbishop of Canterbury, Dr Geoffrey Fisher.

16.   In fact many Serbian Orthodox priests were killed in Croatia and Bosnia by the wartime Ustaše government, and many more by Tito's Partisans. A report compiled by the Synod of the Serbian Orthodox Church after the war gives a breakdown of the figures.

17.   As in the First World War, the Church of England had taken responsibility for training a number of Serbian Orthodox students, this time at Dorchester College (see *Douglas Papers,* Vol. 51, ff. 383ff). However the number involved was much less than the 200 suggested by Bishop Nikolai. Dorchester College had originally been a training college for Anglican missionaries.

18.   Bishop Nikolai's meaning is not quite clear here. Possibly the '100 outside' refers to inmates of the D.P. camps.

19.   The meeting of the Provisional Committee set up to arrange the first assembly of the World Council of Churches; this committee met in February, 1946 (see George Bell, *The Kingship of Christ,* pp. 47ff.).

20.   A reference to the first post-war Lambeth Conference, which met in 1948 (see Jasper, *George Bell,* pp. 348-9).

*so Church Heads (should) too. He wants the Church to
speak. He would like to come to Geneva in February.*

*Church mission of England to Serbia (All Churches).[21]
Very valuable if 5 or 7 came and were seen by people - they
would see some M.P.s, churchmen.[22] People would see they
were not abandoned by England.'*

It would seem that in this conversation, Bishop Nikolai's
characteristic, deeply Christian 'optimism' (about which he had
spoken in his sermon preached at St Luke's Camberwell, in
November 1927)[23] was overshadowed by more sombre prophetic
feelings. In this respect, he and George Bell had been very simi-
larly affected by the events and consequences of the Second
World War. There is also a close parallel between Bishop
Nikolai's plea for the need to distinguish between the majority
of 'Christian Slavs' and the small minority of Communists who
controlled their government, and George Bell's insistence (during
the war) on the need to distinguish between the Nazis and the
mass of the German people. And in both cases these were not
pleas which most people wanted to hear at that time (perhaps
even now Bishop Nikolai's plea sometimes falls on deaf ears). So
this meeting must have touched deep chords in the feelings of
both men; and this shared experience could have deepened and
enriched their friendship; this is clear from their subsequent
correspondence, right up to the end of their lives.

Bishop Nikolai had already decided after his visit to England that
he would go to America - ostensibly because he was not satisfied
with some aspects of the adminstration of Bishop Dionisije, the
head of the Serbian Orthodox Church in the USA.[24] However,

21. Presumably Bishop Nikolai means here that such a mission should not be limited
    to members of the Church of England.
22. Again, Bishop Nikolai's meaning (or Bell's rendering of it) is rather obscure;
    probably he had in mind visiting M.P.s who were Christians.
23. See above, p. 31.
24. Slijepčević, *Istorija*, III, p. 78. Bishop Dionisije Milivojević was Serbian
    Orthodox Bishop of USA and ...

he was probably hoping to make plans to settle there, and had probably even discussed these with George Bell. Certainly, immediately after the conversation recorded in his *Diary*, Bell took steps to see that Bishop Nikolai had introductions to Church leaders in the USA who could help him to organise his life there. On November 17th, 1945 (the day after his meeting with Bishop Nikolai) he wrote the following letter to Bishop Dun of the American Episcopalian Church:

> *This is to introduce you to my dear friend Bishop Nicholai Velimirović from Yugoslavia. I have known him intimately for thirty years, first of all during the First World War, when he was much in England, and ever since, though our personal contact has been continuously interrupted.*
>
> *He is now on his way to the United States. His whole soul is for religion. I have told him that I am sure that you would be most happy to receive him, if he would write to you when he comes. This is to ask you to treat him as a friend, and see him and talk with him.* '[25]

The same day he also wrote to Dr H. S. Leiper in New York, asking him to give Bishop Nikolai 'any help in your power when he comes to the United States ... He will be leaving England any day now.[26] I have told him to get in touch with you direct.' In addition he wrote to the Archbishop of Canterbury,[27] and to Dr Visser't Hooft (General Secretary of the Provisional Committee of the World Council of Churches), asking that Bishop Nikolai should be invited to the forthcoming meeting of the Provisional Committee in Geneva. Then he wrote to Bishop Nikolai, to inform him about these letters which he had written on his

---

24. contd. ... Canada from 1939 to 1963. In 1964 he was unfrocked by the Serbian Council of Bishops as the leader of a breakaway Serbian Orthodox Church. He died in 1979, as Metropolitan of the diocese of Nova Gračanica.
25. *Bell Papers*, Vol. 79, f. 131.
26. *Ibid.*, f. 134.
27. *Ibid.*, f. 132.

behalf. At the end of the letter he said: 'I cannot tell you how deeply moved I was by our talk yesterday, and what a joy it was to be with you.'[28]

Bishop Nikolai replied to this letter on November 22nd, 1945. First he thanked Bishop Bell for writing the letters of introduction to his American friends, and also (in a postscript) for a copy of his biography of Archbishop Randall Davidson; then he went on to comment on the state of spiritual confusion in the Christian nations, especially those of the European continent, and the universal anguish of human souls, all over the world. At the end of this letter he writes:

> *I am going today to the country, on doctor's advice, in order to recuperate a little my physical health, and wait for the first available overseas transport. Walsingham's monastery has been recommended to me.'[29]*

Bishop Nikolai's first letter to George Bell from the USA is dated February 6th, 1946, and addressed from the College of Preachers attached to Washington Cathedral, Washington DC; in this letter his characteristic optimism seems to have revived.

My dear Bishop and Friend,
The Lord's grace be with you!
*   You see where I am - after Dachau in Preachers' College in Washington! Like a fairy tale, and yet dramatic reality. How wonderful are the Lord's dealings with men!*

---

28. *Ibid.*, f. 135.

29. *Ibid.*, f. 136. Bishop Nikolai does not say who it was who recommended him to go to Walsingham. There was a Serbian Orthodox priest, Dr Dimitrije Najdanović, resident there after the Second World War (see Colin Stephenson, *Walsingham Way*, p. 200); but he could not have been there in 1945, as he was then teaching at Dorchester College.

Here I have found all as you described to me. Bishop Dun, Dr Wedel and all the rest of their brothers and collabo-rators in this holy house are very, very kind people indeed. I did not write to you before I see Lord Halifax.[30] *I saw him today. He is just what I thought of him and all you said he would be. A God's servant with a gentleman's manner. As long as you have him and two or three similar to him among your leading statesmen, do not be afraid about England's security.*

Now here I see an urgent two-fold task for one who is more capable than me: to call thise [these] people to a spiritual awakening (and spiritual discipline) lest they sink into self-sufficiency and pride,[31] *and impress on them the most imperative need of their close friendship with England. Please, send someone over here to do this work.*

As to Geneva's conference, I am not going there. No invitation received.[32] *Please do explain my little proposal*[33] *to the council if it should be mentioned in Geneva. And if you should ever there have need for some information about my country, you may call Dr Moatchanin at the Red Cross. Another man who can impartially give you many informations about Austria, Bavaria, South Germany (which you did not reach during your trip to Germany),*[34] *and also in Russia is Dr Bruschweiler. His father [is] a Protestant pastor and mother a Russian. I met him in Salzburg.*[35] *He is General Secretary of a*

---

30. Bell had tried to arrange a meeting between Bishop Nikolai and Lord Halifax during Bishop Nikolai's recent visit to England (see *Bell Papers*, Vol. 79, f. 133).
31. When Bishop Nikolai visited America in 1927, he had been favourably impressed by the spiritual vitality of the people he met (see above, p. 34). Now, it seems, he was somewhat disillusioned.
32. Evidently Bell's attempts to secure an invitation for Bishop Nikolai had not succeeded.
33. Possibly a reference to Bishop Nikolai's suggestion that there should be regular meetings of Church leaders.
34. A reference to George Bell's first post-war visit to Germany in October, 1945 (see Jasper, *George Bell*, pp. 293-4).
35. Bishop Nikolai passed through Salzburg on his way to England in the autumn of 1945 (see Slijepčević, *Istorija*, III, p. 76).

committee of displaced persons. He gave me heaps of infor-
mations on this subject. His address too is at the Red Cross.

I read that you are a member of the Oecumenical
Ref[ugee] Commission.[36] *Thank God that such a comission*
had been formed. I am very much troubled about our D.Ps
and refugees. It would certainly be a sin to force them to go
home - to the realm of shadow and death.[37] *May the Lord*
give you light and courage to do in this problem what is best.

I shall pray and pray for Geneva's conference's success
and for you wherever you are and whatever you do. For I
know that you are praying for me.

With brotherly love in our Lord,
            Very sincerely yours,

                    + Bishop Nikolai

This letter, though generally cheerful in tone, does give the
impression that Bishop Nikolai was feeling somewhat frustrated
at not being involved in such activities as the preparations for
the first meeting of the World Council of Churches, and not
being able to alleviate the plight of refugees, especially his com-
patriots. At least it must have been helpful for him to have been
in touch with George Bell, who was directly concerned with such
problems,[38] and to be able to give him some information which
might be useful. It was no doubt a sign of Bishop Nikolai's
restored physical health and unquenchable spiritual vitality that
he continued to be deeply concerned about these problems.

---

36. This was set up by the World Council of Churches in 1946 (see George Bell,
    The Kingship of Christ, p. 114, where he says 'Its special care was for refugees
    of the Protestant and Eastern Orthodox faiths, and for those of no faith at all.'
37. In fact many thousands of Yugoslav refugees were forcibly repatriated, and
    suffered the fate foreseen by Bishop Nikolai (see Michael Lees, *The
    Rape of Serbia*, pp. 304-5).
38. See *The Kingship of Christ*, Chapter 11.

A few days later (on February 8th) he wrote another letter to George Bell, one of the most interesting in their entire correspondence.

My dear Bishop Bell,

I am writing to you again. I have become so forgetful - it is a shame.

In my last letter I forgot to mention to you the Old Catholic Church in Switzerland.[39] The Old Catholic Faculty at the University of Bern was my first alma mater.[40] *The famous E[duard] Herzog[41] was my professor for the New Testament. My other professors were: Michaud, Thözcings, Walker, Kunz and others - all great champions of Old Catholicism. The present bishop Küzy was then Pfarrer of Basel. Among my fellow students were amongst others: Gilg, Bailly, Seiler. All the three alive.[42] Dr Arnold Gilg has become famous. He was for a period Rector of the University. Bailly and Seiler are parish priests still, as they were from the beginning, convinced Christians and good pastors.*

Now what I wish to say is a suggestion that it would be a very good deed if you would pay a visit to them in Bern, to see their theological faculty and to preach in their church there (Hertzergasse).[43] It would of course be of greater effect if His Grace the Archbishop of Canterbury, together with

---

39. See C. B. Moss, *The Old Catholic Movement*, Chapter XVIII.

40. I have been unable to trace the circumstances leading up to Bishop Nikolai's studies in Berne. It was the custom of the Old Catholics to invite representatives of other Churches to their annual conferences, and a visitor from the Serbian Orthodox Church was present at their Reunion Conference at Bonn in 1875 (see Moss, *op. cit.*, p. 267). This visit might have led to an on-going connection between the two Churches.

41. One of the first professors at the Old Catholic Theological Faculty in Berne, established in 1874 (Moss, *op. cit.*, p. 253).

42. This sentence suggests that Bishop Nikolai had been able to keep in touch with these fellow-students.

43. The Christ Catholic (i.e. Old Catholic) Church of St Peter and St Paul in Berne, still active.

*you, would do that. They would certainly rejoice. And it
would strengthen that tenacious little flock of Christ. And it
would also tighten the relations between your Church and
theirs.*[44] *I really think it would be a blessed work. I know they
have got a parish at Geneva and Lausanne, Lucern, etc. but
Bern is their Metropolia.*

Most probably you yourself planned to do that.[45] *In that
case, well. I am only seconding your good intention. And I do
it because I love these wonderful people of God, as I love my
own.*
Wishing to you and His Grace bon voyage *for Switzerland
and praying for a real success of your labor, I remain as
always,*

> *With brotherly love in our blessed Lord,*
> *Yours,*
> *+ Bishop Nikolai* [46]

It would seem from this letter that Bishop Nikolai was not
aware of the fact that the Old Catholic and Anglican Churches
had for some time been in full communion.[47] George Bell had
not been personally concerned in this particular aspect of inter-
Church relations; hence it is not so surprising that he and Bishop
Nikolai had not discussed it. The interesting point about this letter
is the fact that Bishop Nikolai wished to share with his friend his
own continuing affection for his theological *alma mater,* still so
strong so many years after he studied there.

Several months elapsed before Bishop Nikolai next wrote to
George Bell, on December 17th, 1946. This letter was written

---

44. Relations between the Church of England and the Old Catholics were in fact
    close and cordial; since 1931 the two Churches have been in full communion.

45. There is no evidence in Jasper's biography that George Bell's many and varied
    ecclesiastical activities included contact with the Old Catholics.

46. *Bell Papers,* Vol. 79, ff. 140-42.

47. See Moss, *op. cit.,* Ch. XXVIII.

from the Serbian Orthodox Monastery of St Sava in Libertyville, Illinois, which was to be Bishop Nikolai's headquarters for the rest of his life, though he paid frequent visits to the Russian Monastery in South Canaan, near New York, and in fact died there. It is a very long letter,[48] mainly about the plight of Serbian displaced persons. It begins with a Christmas greeting:

My dear friend Bishop George,
*   ... Christ the Messiah is born,*
*   ... Verily He is born.*

I greet you with this habitual Christmas greeting of our Eastern Church. The meaning of this greeting is that the expected Messiah has come to save the world, and that we ought not to look for another. Jesus Christ the Victor, the Invincible!

*   Armed with this positive faith our little and tragic Serbian people endured, as you know, the Mohammedan oppression, the Austrian tyranny,[49] the Nazis' merciless rule, and are now enduring the ruthless persecution of organised world atheism.*

*   Their suffering at home in Yugoslavia under the enemies of Christ is at least comprehensible. But it is wholly incomprehensible that they should suffer under the so-called Christian and Democratic English. I think of the so-called D. Ps in the prison camps in Germany. If some other gentlemen were the head of the British government, and the British army of pagan mind, and not those deeply-convinced Christians like*

---

48. *Bell Papers,* Vol. 79., ff. 143-44; unlike most of Bishop Nikolai's letters, this one is typed.

49. Most of Serbia had never actually been under Austrian rule (apart from the Vojvodina); however, during the years immediately before the First World War, Austrian (i.e. Habsburg) foreign policy was consistently hostile to Serbia. There were also many Serbs living under Habsburg rule in Bosnia-Hercegovina and Croatia.

Mr Attlee and (Field) Marshal Montgomery, it would not be astonishing at all. But ...

I am not intending to describe to you their situation, according to our informations, their privations, severe restrictions, humiliations of every kind, and their everyday fear of being kidnapped, and moreover forcible separation of officers from men, all in order to please the 'Red Allies'. I hope it might be somewhat exaggerated; would [to] God that it is so. But if it were half true, it would be too much.

Knowing the noble and humane character of the English, it is very hard for me to take all their complaints as accurate.

Therefore I beg to ask from you only one thing in God's name. Do send one of your Bishops (as the Archbishop did send one once to Belgrade)[50] to see those Serbs in the camps of Sendwarden, Verde, and down to Munich, to talk with our chaplains, officers and men in order to get [a] true picture and verify the facts. Just as you yourself did when you travelled in Germany.[51]

There are over twenty organisations helping the recovery and welfare of the Germans which I heartily approve. For the German people as a whole must not be considered guilty on account of their lunatic leaders.[52]

There are also powerful Jewish organisations helping the Jewish DPs, and the Catholic helping Catholics, etc. But there is no organisation in the world that I know helping the helpless Serbs in exile. Beside[s], many Englishmen are travelling in Germany, but none looks into those Lagers where thousands and thousands of Serbian soldiers are

---

50. This might possibly refer to the Anglican mission to the Serbian Orthodox Church in the spring of 1940 (see above, p. 58).

51. This probably refers to Bell's second post-war visit to Germany, in June, 1946 (see Jasper, *George Bell*, pp. 300ff).

52. Bishop Nikolai is here expressing similar views to those which made George Bell unpopular in some quarters during the Second World War.

languishing in despair. They write: 'We hoped very much in the Anglican Church, but she failed us.'[53]

I am not accusing, nor am I complaining. Those suffering Serbs are not my sons, but Christ's, for Christ died for them, not me. You know that Christ is more with those that suffer than with those that incur suffering (Lazarus and the dive [sic].[54] *But I am filled with fear for England, which is a bulwark against evil forces of anti-Christ. For you know from the Book of Life how our God in His anger may terrible [terribly] punish a whole nation because of the innocent blood of one single man. For here is the life of myriads in question, and not of one man.*

Now you see that I am not writing to you as an advocate. No. I experienced how a human soul, while abandoned by all the world, is wonderfully tied up with Christ. Such experience have my Christian countrymen in Germany, being in camps for six years. I am informed that there is a marvelous spiritual awakening among them. I am proud of them. They all asked for Bibles, and I succeeded through the American Bible Society to send them Bibles. But that is not the only thing they need.

Not yet as an advocate, I say, but as a friend I write to you, an old friend and as a weaker brother to stronger one. As you remember, we both as young priests grew for years, and developed our character under the guidance of that wonderful Christian wizard, the late Archbishop Randall [Davidson], God bless his soul.[55] *His living spirit is still uniting us from the Higher World. I feel it.*

---

53. Presumably it was the letters he received from Serbian D.Ps which provided Bishop Nikolai with information about their plight.
54. The story of Lazarus and the Rich Man (Dives) in Luke 16:19-31.
55. Archbishop Randall Davidson took a strong personal interest in the young Fr Nikolai during the First World War, and evidently thought highly of him (see above, p. 13).

I hoped to see you in this country, with the present Archbishop,[56] to tell you about this matter, of which I [am] loath to write, unless compelled by conscience. But you did not come, and I felt destitute and poor.

Finally I can only repeat the word of the Blessed Gospel - 'If you can do anything ...' (Mark 9:22). If you send a real Christian to those camps, he will bring you a truthful report, which you can use as the Spirit of God will tell you, either in the Church or in the House of Lords.

All the glory of the Poor One of Bethlehem who made us all rich, and to the salvation of the English people.

Wishing a happy Christmas to you, to Mrs Bell and to your people, I remain,

Very devotedly yours,
+Bishop Nikolai

It must surely have rejoiced Bishop Nikolai's heart to receive a prompt reply to this letter; and the content of the reply must have re-assured him, indicating as it does that George Bell shared his concern about the Yugoslav displaced persons and that he was taking steps to try to improve their conditions. George Bell's letter, dated January 3rd, 1947 begins:

My dear brother in Christ
and dearest friend,

Thank you very much for your letter and for your Christmas greeting. I have continually thought of you, and not least since our long talk in London, and I warmly reciprocate the Christmas greeting and the Epiphany greeting too.

That you should have written about the sufferings of the Yugoslavians now in prison camps outside their country just

---

56. Archbishop Fisher first visited the USA in 1946, in order to attend the General Convention of the Episcopalian Church in Philadelphia (see W. Purcell, *Fisher of Lambeth*, pp. 175-6).

at this time is a strange coincidence, for I had also raised the question of the suffering Yugoslavs as displaced persons in the House of Lords. I enclose an account of the debate herewith. I know that speeches are little: but the Bishop of Gibraltar has for many months now been doing his best. Your letter comes with exceptional urgency. I hope that all you say is not fully true - though it certainly does need enquiry.

I am taking up immediately the possibility of sending an Anglican bishop to see the Serbs in the camps you name, and talking with your chaplains and officers and men. I know that you write to me as an old friend, and I appreciate this very much. I appreciate too your appeal to that wonderful old Christian, Randall Davidson. I will do whatever I can and will write to you again.

I am hoping to be in New York in the latter half of April, to attend meetings of the World Council.[57] Perhaps then it will be possible for us to meet: God grant it.

With brotherly affection,[58]
(George Bell)

The same day Bishop Bell wrote to Herbert Waddams, Secretary to the Church of England Council for Foreign Relations, asking him to take up the problem of the Yugoslav Displaced Persons with the Archbishop of Canterbury; and some days later he also wrote to General Heathcote-Smith, the officer in charge of Displaced Persons' camps in the British zone, requesting information about the location of camps in which different nationalities were settled.[59] The reply he received was moderately re-assuring; he was told that the conditions 'had improved to an

---

57. There is no indication, either in George Bell's *Papers*, or in his biography, that he did actually go to New York in April, 1947.

58. *Bell Papers*, Vol. 79, ff. 145-6.

59. *Bell Papers*, Vol. 79, ff. 147-50.

appreciable degree', and that Bishop Nikolai's letter referred to conditions existing a month or two previously.[60]

After this exchange of letters, there is a gap of about four years when there does not appear to have been any direct communication between the two friends. However, during this period George Bell was offered the Order of Saint Joanikije in recognition of his services to the Serbian Orthodox Church. This was an Order recently established by the Council of the Serbian Orthodox Diocese of America and Canada to commemorate the six hundreth anniversary of the establishment of the Serbian Patriarchate in 1346.[61] It seems probable that Bishop Nikolai was in some way involved in this offer being made to George Bell. The Order was also offered to the Archbishop of Canterbury.[62]

George Bell's letter of acceptance, dated February 9th, 1948, and addressed to Bishop Dionisije, reflects the continuing warmth of his feelings both for the Serbian Orthodox Church and for Bishop Nikolai personally:

My dear Lord Bishop,
I am most touched by your most kind letter of 22nd January, in which you generously offer me the Order of S. Joanikije, made by your Diocese in commemoration of the 600th Anniversary of the creation of the Serbian Patriarchate. Last week the Order itself arrived in Chichester.[63]

---

60. *Ibid.,* f. 150.

61. In 1345 the Serbian ruler Stefan Dušan was proclaimed Emperor of the Serbs and Greeks, after a series of successful military campaigns during which he overran and occupied large areas of the enfeebled Byzantine Empire. The following year, the Archbishop of the autocephalous Serbian Orthodox Church, Joannicius (Joanikije) II, was raised to the rank of Patriarch.

62. *Bell Papers,* Vol. 79, f. 152.

63. The actual symbol of the Order was a specially-designed cross. Possibly this is the cross which George Bell is wearing in the photographs facing the frontispiece and p. 133 in Jasper's biography.

> *I need not say with what pleasure and gratitude I accept the Order and how proud I am to have it. My love for the Serbian Church began more than thirty years ago, and my care for it, and my friends within it, notably my oldest friend of all in the Serbian Church, Bishop Nikolai, will be life-long.*
>
> *With prayers for the Serbian Church and for yourself and your diocese,*
>
>

I remain,

Your faithful brother and servant in Christ,[64]

(George Bell)

>

George Bell was very busy at this time with activities connected with the inauguration of the World Council of Churches; these included a good deal of travelling and also a considerable load of administrative work, in addition to his routine duties as a diocesan bishop.[65] He was concerned about the lack of interest in the World Council in the Church of England as a whole; and in order to try and counteract this he wrote a short account of the movement leading up to the establishment of the World Council, under the title *The Kingship of Christ*.[66] This book was written under the pressure of a very tight deadline. A life so packed with activity could not have left much time for private correspondence, so it is not surprising that no letters to Bishop Nikolai have survived from this time.

Bishop Nikolai, although he was no longer in the mainstream of ecclesiastical administration or inter-Church relations (a fact which perhaps still irked him at times) was also busy in a variety of ways. As well as trying to improve the conditions of the Yugoslav Displaced Persons' camps, he occupied himself with

---

64. *Bell Papers*, Vol. 79, f. 253.
65. See Jasper, *George Bell*, Chapter 16.
66. *Ibid.*, p. 331. *The Kingship of Christ*, which is lucidly planned and beautifully written, remains an excellent guide to the early history of the World Council of Churches.

raising funds for the Serbian Orthodox Church in London,[67] and also continued his writing. This consisted mainly of hymns and sermons; and in 1951 he produced one of his finest works: *The Life of St Sava*. This work, written in English, is not only a biography of the saint, but also a meditation on its significance. In spite of his exile, and his anxiety about the evil effects of communism, he seems to have recovered something of his former characteristic buoyancy of spirit;[68] this is reflected in a letter written in 1948 to Canon Douglas:

> *My dear Canon Douglas,*
>   *Do you believe in telepathy?*
> *I was just talking about you with a Serbian friend, Mr Doychinovich who met you in London, and behold; your letter with a wonderful photograph of your spiritualized face dropped into my hands.*
>
> *Those who honour my friends honour me. Therefore I am grateful to the Council of London University for having honoured you so deservedly.[69]*
>
> *How are you? And how is your cheerful brother Charles, my friend?*
>
> *Yesterday I felt some good old England while listening to a sermon by Duncan Tokes in St John's Cathedral.[70] He spoke very strongly against [the] 'incarnation of evil', meaning communism.*
>
> *Please, if you can, find some channel (and I am sure that you can) to express my deep personal gratitude to your government for admitting some thousands of our long-suffering Serbs into England. The prophets of old used to say to their people: 'the remnant will be saved.' And we are praying to God to make England his tool to save some remnant of a*

---

67. The Serbian Orthodox Church of St Sava, founded in 1942.
68. See above, pp. 69, 73.
69. It is not clear what this honour was; Bishop Nikolai could be referring to Canon Douglas's office as Chairman of Convocation in London University.
70. St John's Episcopalian Cathedral in New York.

twice-crucified people in this war for faithfulness to the Allies. Would you ask Charles if he could find a a copy of my Spiritual Rebirth of Europe?[71] *I would be most thankful.*

And now, my dear friend, be cheerful. It was prophesied long before that satanic atheism will get the mortal blow in Serbia. Do not doubt this. But pray for your Serbs in misery. And try to give some consolation to those who are in England.

Very sincerely yours,

+ Bishop Nikolai[72]

Early in 1952, Bishop Nikolai visited England once more (for the last time), for the consecration of the Serbian Orthodox Church in London, dedicated to St Sava. This provided an opportunity for a reunion with his English friends, including George Bell. One result of this was a resumption of their corre-spon-dence, which seems to have lapsed for some years. On December 20th, 1952, George Bell wrote to Bishop Nikolai informing him, among other things, of the death of Bishop Irinej Đorđević.[73] Bishop Nikolai replied in a letter dated January 1st, 1953, addressed from the office of the *Glasnik Sv. Save* (St Sava Herald)[74] in New York. He begins with New Year greetings:

My dear Brother Bishop George,

Happy New Year to you, your flock and all England - all through 365 days.

Only yesterday reached me here yours of 20th December. Yes, our dear Bishop Iriney passed away, more embittered by

---

71. See above, Chapter II, p. 17.

72. *Douglas Papers,* Vol. 51, f. 205. This is the only postwar letter from Bishop Nikolai in this volume of the *Douglas Papers.*

73. There is unfortunately no copy of this letter from George Bell among his papers. However it is not surprising that he mentioned the death of Bishop Irinej, since he died in Cambridge in August, 1952.

74. A fortnightly journal published by the Serbian Orthodox Church in the USA.

*the Serbs than by the English.[75] God bless his soul. Unselfish
and courageous was he.*

*No wonder that you are troubled by Tito. I am glad that
the Church of England is not responsible for bringing him to
power.[76] It happens so, that the Church has to atone for the
sins of politicians. Your Church, and ours too. Our Orthodox
Church in Yugoslavia is the only remained backbone of the
Serbian people. And the atheists are trying to break that
backbone. I know that you and H.G. the Archbishop[77] are
worrying about it. Thank you. We shall pray. But let Mr
Churchill look to it first of all. Six years ago I spoke to him
on 'Queen Elizabeth' of Tito, and he said: 'What can I do
now I am no longer in power?' Well, now he is in power.[78]*

*It is too late now to give you any suggestions what the
W.C. of Churches could do at the conference at Lucknow.[79]
Shortly, to insist on sending the help, but if this definitely
blocked, then publicly protest.[80] The people in England
should be informed.*

*I intend to come to E.[England], but not being an
American citizen it is difficult without a special reason or
invitation.*

*I hear that a nasty propaganda is going on among the
Serb D.Ps in England, either to become British citizens, or to*

---

75. Irinej Đorđević was one of the Serbian ordinands who studied in England
during the First World War. Later he became Orthodox Bishop of Šibenik in
Dalmatia.

76. Some people in Yugoslavia were of the opinion that Churchill was at least partly
responsible for Tito's rise to political power (I personally encountered this
when I worked in the country from 1956-66).

77. A reference to Geoffrey Fisher, then Archbishop of Canterbury.

78. Churchill was Prime Minister in the Conservative government which was
returned to power after the election of 1951.

79. A reference to the meeting of the Central Committee of the World Council of
Churches at Lucknow, during December, 1952 and January, 1953 (see *The
Kingship of Christ*, pp. 92-3).

80. It is not clear what Bishop Nikolai is referring to here.

go home. (A certain gentleman Kulman).[81] *Rev. Nikolić*[82] *may say more about it. Please, do what you can to let Serbs in peace at least in your country. And I am sure God will recompense such a faith in His own unexpected way.*

And now let us have adamant faith in the Lord, and pray constantly for each other.

With affectionate greetings,
Yours brotherly in Christ,
+Bishop Nicholai [83]

This was the last letter that Bishop Nikolai wrote to George Bell (or at any rate the last which has been preserved among Bell's papers). However, they did meet once more, when George Bell came to America in August, 1954 for the Second General Assembly of the World Council of Churches at Evanston, Illinois.[84] In fact they met twice: first on August 22nd, when Bishop Nikolai made a special visit to Evanston to see his friend, and again after the conference, when George Bell visited Bishop Nikolai in his monastery, at his invitation. Later George Bell commented on this visit: 'He was then old and frail, with sorrow in his heart.'[85] This was their last personal contact before Bishop Nikolai died, on March 18th, 1956.

There were immediate reactions to the news of Bishop Nikolai's death - in America, where he had made his home shortly after the end of the Second World War; in his native country, though he had not been there since his hurried departure to Dachau in the autumn of 1944; and in England, which he had visited so many times, and had so many friends. In England there

---

81. Presumably 'a certain Kulman' was the person responsible for spreading these rumours.
82. The Rector of the Serbian Orthodox Church of St Sava.
83. *Bell Papers*, Vol. 79, f. 155.
84. See Jasper, *George Bell*, pp. 333-6.
85. *Bell Papers*, Vol. 79, f. 235.

were many tributes from leaders of different Churches, especially to his gifts as a preacher; in this respect he was compared to such eminent Anglican divines as Bishop Gore and Dr Henry Scott-Holland.[86] Also a short biographical pamphlet was published, written by Stephen Graham.

George Bell's final tribute to his friend was a sermon preached at a memorial service for Bishop Nikolai, held in the Serbian Orthodox Church of St Sava in London on September 22nd, 1956. It is a remarkable sermon, powerfully expressing his deep feeling and understanding for his friend, and is here reproduced in full.

> *In the Church of St Sava we meet for prayer and reflection on the death of a saint. When Bishop Nikolai Velimirović died on March 18th this year in the Monastery of St Sava, South Canaan in the United States, a great wave of mourning began which reached beyond the diocese of Žiča. When the news of his death was announced in Belgrade, all the bells of the churches in the city tolled simultaneously. Everywhere in Yugoslavia his passing was felt as a heavy blow, and wherever Serbs are found in distant continents, in camps or any kind of exile, their hearts are stirred. Nor was it only Serbs who lamented a dear father and leader, but inumerable believers of the Orthodox Communion and friends of many nations and Churches throughout the world. To use Bishop Nikolai's own beautiful words at the end of his* Life of St Sava, *'The death of a member of a family is a blow to that family. The death of a King or a national hero is a blow to his nation. But the death of a saint is a blow to many nations, even to the world. For a true saint is like heavenly ozone to weaker human souls.'*[87]

---

86. *Ibid.*, f. 265.
87. Nikolai Velimirović, *The Life of St Sava*, p. 149. The text actually reads: 'like heavenly fresh air to weaker human souls'.

There is a peculiar fitness in the holding of a memorial service in England, for he loved England and its people only less dearly than his own homeland, and throughout his life did everything in his power to deepen and strengthen the links between the Orthodox Churches and the Churches of this country.

Nikolai Velimirović was born in Lelić, in central Serbia on the 23rd of December, 1880. After education in a village school, and then in gymnasije, in Belgrade and St Petersburg and Berne,[88] he became a professor in the Belgrade Academy of Theology. He was a master of many languages, and held doctorates in Divinity and Philosophy.[89] He was already famous throughout Serbia as a preacher when he came to London in 1915, at the call of the Serbian government.[90] He preached in many pulpits up and down the country, and was the first minister not belonging to the Anglican Communion to preach in St Paul's Cathedral and Westminster Abbey. His special task was the promotion of the Serbian Relief Fund,[91] and the interpretation of his country and his country's faith to the statesmen and churchmen of England, through books[92] as well as through the spoken word, and incidentally the supervision of the training of Serbian students under Church of England auspices for the ministry of the Serbian Orthodox Church.[93]

I had much to do with him in those days, and have vivid memories of his visits to Canterbury and Lambeth. I recall

---

88. This passage, as it stands, is misleading, since the *gimnazija* in Yugoslavia represents the secondary stage of education; in fact Bishop Nikolai's studies at St Petersburg and Berne were at post-graduate level.

89. Bishop Nikolai referred to his study of philosophy in Germany in his sermon preached at St Luke's, Camberwell in 1927 (see above, p. 30).

90. When Belgrade fell to the Germans in 1915, the Serbian government moved first to Niš, then later to Corfu.

91 See *The Making of a New Europe*, pp. 163-4, 221.

92. See Appendix I, p. 101. See above, pp. xi-xii, 7.

93. See above, pp. 9-11.

*the strong links of reverence and friendship which bound the
young Fr Nikolai to the old Archbishop of Canterbury,
Randall Davidson. He said to me many years later, 'He was
like a father to me. He took me to his heart.'*[94] *The first time
Fr Nikolai came to the Old Palace, Canterbury, to stay the
night, it was with a shock that he found himself summoned
by a constable to come and report as an alien at the local
police station. 'I thought', he said 'that the Archbishop of
Canterbury was the greatest man in England after the King.
But I have found that the Law is greater.'*

*I remember also how, as 'your Grace's minor brother in
Christ', he pleaded with the Archbishop to support his
scheme for theological students, and was somewhat dismayed
to discover that the Archbishop wanted much more than at
the moment he was able to give him, by way of chapter and
verse, or the authority under which this scheme would come.
'Nothing,' wrote Fr Nikolai in a letter to me*[95] *from the
Serbian Information Bureau in June, 1917, 'nothing is so very
precise in this time of universal chaos. And I am afraid our
poor Archbishop of Serbia is not speaking very clearly and
precisely as to the Serbian theological students ... We have
now got 11 Serbian students of theology. They are very good
material. All the responsibility for any action I will take on
myself. Don't be afraid of anything. Either the Church will
awake during this war, or never. It is an exceptional time.' It is
unnecessary to say that Fr Nikolai prevailed.*[96]

*Soon after the First World War, he returned to Serbia. In
1919, he was consecrated Bishop of Žiča, just 700 years after
the consecration of St Sava as first Archbishop of Serbia in
1219*[97] *with his throne at Žiča where, after his installation, on*

---

94. See above, p. 68.
95. This letter is quoted in full in George Bell's biography of Archbishop
    Randall Davidson.
96. See above, p. 9.
97. The consecration of St Sava as Archbishop of Serbia in 1219 marked the
    beginning of the autocephalous Serbian Orthodox Church, since
    thereafter the Archbishop was chosen by the bishops of that Church,
    and not by the Patriarch of Constantinople.

the Feast of the Ascension in 1220, he crowned his brother Stephen as the First Serbian King. In 1920, Bishop Nikolai was transferred to the diocese of Ochrid. But in 1936 he left Ochrid and returned to his old diocese of Žiča - and, though in exile, held the bishopric until his death.[98]

As Bishop, he exercised an extraordinary influence on the whole of Yugoslavia by his spiritual leadership, his teaching and preaching, his books, his care for the clergy and the young, his deep interest in vital religious movements, his moral and intellectual genius and imagination, combined with a remarkable gift for writing in language which could be understood by the simplest people. He was both a seer and a man of prayer. No one who saw him celebrating the Liturgy, as I did once, in the open air, side by side with Bishop Irinej [Ćirić] of Novi Sad,[99] *in the midst of many thousands of Serbian people, gathered from all over the countryside, and afterwards moving through the great company, blessing men, women and children, could be in any doubt of the greatness of his devotion to his Lord, or the love of his flock for their shepherd.*

During the period between the wars, he again visited England on various occasions. But he saw very clearly the threats of inhumanity, atheism and war which were hanging over Europe. His strong convictions as to right and wrong, united with a fervent patriotism, made him a convinced and uncompromising opponent of the National Socialist creed and the Nazis when they attacked and occupied Yugoslavia during the Second World War. In 1941 he was arrested. He was kept for four years as a prisoner, and spent fourteen months of that time with Patriarch Gavrilo in the concentration

---

98. Bishop Nikolai remained the titular Bishop of Žiča until his death (see Slipjepčević, *Istorija*, III, p. 251).

99. Presumably this liturgy was celebrated during the meeting of the executive committee of the Universal Council for Life and Work which took place in Novi Sad in September, 1933 (see above, p. 36).

Bishop George Bell

Chichester Cathedral - a sketch by James Chrismas

camp at Dachau.[100] *He was set free by the American army in 1945.*[101] *But with Yugoslavia under Communist domination and subject to the doctrine and practice of the Communist system, with its rejection of the rule of God, he was destined never again to see his native land. He was very sad at all his country had to endure. He warned his friends in many nations against an easy acceptance of a new kind of pan-Slavism preached from Moscow. But he had a passionate belief in the vitality of the Orthodox faith, and the full restoration of the Church in God's good time.*

In the autumn of 1945, he came to England for the christening of King Peter's son Alexander by the Patriarch in Westminster Abbey.[102] *He had changed greatly. He was worn, rather spare, with a beard more grey than black, and clearly suffering. His body, he said was weak, but his spirit well. Amongst the places he visited was the city of Chichester, where the Patriarch and he were received in the cathedral.*[103]

A little time after that I had a talk with him about many things.[104] *He had an intense concern for the deepening of the religion of democratic statesmen. He would like to see a world conference of Churches which would speak like this:'We praise you for your democracy. It is good. It is founded on Christian principles. But it is not enough. You need to turn to God.' He mentioned Christian statesmen in Britain and France, and the great importance of statesmen being Christians, and of the public at large encouraging them.*

---

100. Actually this is not correct; Patriarch Gavrilo and Bishop Nikolai spent less than six months in Dachau.

101. This too is not quite correct: the two Church leaders were released before the arrival of the American army (see above, p. 63). Slijepčević's account is confirmed by the record of Bishop Nikolai's conversation with George Bell in November 1945, preserved in Bell's diary.

102. The christening took place in a private chapel of the Abbey.

103 Presumably it was George Bell who invited Patriarch Gavrilo and Bishop Nikolai to Chichester, and arranged for their official reception in the cathedral.

104. A reference to the meeting of the two bishops in November, 1945.

He also spoke of how people could encourage their country, especially by prayer. And as to his own years of imprisonment in concentration camps, he spoke of God's presence with him in prison, of the angels, and of his real experience of God's care and love. Suffering (he said) had taught him what nothing else could have done.

He visited England once more in 1952, for the consecration of this church. It was one of the most memorable occasions, for Serbs in this country, since the end of the war. I spoke with him again then. But for the last ten and a half years of his life, while his name was a household word in his own land, his physical home was in the United States. And the last time I saw him was at Evanston, Illinois,[105] where he came from the monastery of St Sava in Libertyville, in the same state, to talk to me, with a young priest, on August 22nd, 1954. He was aged and frail, with sorrow in his heart. Although he himself had to go to New York almost at once, he asked me to visit his monastery when the World Council of Churches Assembly was over, and so I went there from Evanston and saw the place where he lived and worked. I can therefore imagine the place where his body lies buried.[106]

'The death of a member of a family is a blow to that family. The death of a king or a hero is a blow to his nation. But the death of a saint is a blow to many nations or even to the world. For a true saint is like heavenly ozone to weaker human souls.' Yes, the personality and example Bishop Nikolai is like heavenly ozone to weaker human souls. We little men are so busy and so blind. 'Late and soon, getting and spending, we lay waste our powers.' In the midst of all the noise and traffic, the conflict of politics and the wars of nations, he always stood for the eternal.

---

105. This was when George Bell went to Evanston for the second General Assembly of the WCC in August, 1954 (see Jasper, *George Bell*, pp. 333-5).
106. Bishop Nikolai's remains have now been removed to his birthplace in Serbia.

A marvellous man, yes. A great patriot, yes. But he was more than that. He was a prophet of God, not only of God's mercy, but of God's judgment.

Let my final words be words which Bishop Nikolai wrote to me from New York in November 1945: 'The Lord's peace be with you ... The spiritual confusion of Christian nations especially those of the European continent, and the universal anguish of human souls all over the world cannot be clarified, refreshed and finally healed by anyone but Christ Himself. The gentle voice of our Saviour: 'Without me ye can do nothing' sounds like the thundering of the last trumpet in my ears, and I am sure in the ears of myriads of simple Christians amidst the clamour of the world of our time.[107]

George Bell ended his address by making an appeal for a permanent memorial to Bishop Nikolai in London: this was to be a house bearing his name, in which sick and aged Serbs could fined a refuge.[108] 'It would be fitly placed in England, not only because of the great need of the Serbs here in exile, but also as a further sign of the strong ties which bind Bishop Nikolai to his friends here, and another link between the Orthodox Church and the Churches of Britain.'[109]

---

107. See above, p. 71.

108. A printed appeal for such a memorial to Bishop Nikolai had already been circulated (*Bell Papers*, Vol. 79, f.161). The house (Dom Episkopa Nikolaja) now stands beside the Serbian Orthodox Church in west London

109. *Bell Papers*, Vol. 354, ff. 229-36. It is clear that much of the content of this address is drawn from George Bell's account of his conversation with Bishop Nikolai in November, 1945. This conversation left a deep impression on him, as he said on more than one occasion.

EPILOGUE

George Bell's address at this memorial service made a powerful impact on his hearers, as can be seen from the following letters. The first, dated September 24th, 1956, is from Fr. Miloje Nikolić,[1] then the Rector of the Serbian Orthodox Church of St Sava in London:

My first duty is to send you a letter, but I really don't know how to begin it, being still under the deepest impression of the way in which you paid a tribute to our late Bishop. It was indeed the most moving address I have ever heard, and the warmest tribute ever paid by an Englishman to a Serb, by one of the highest prelates of the Church of England to a Prince of the Serbian Orthodox Church. The late Bishop really was a 'Prophet of God', and his death, as you rightly said, was 'the death of a saint', a blow to many nations even the world. Bishop Nikolai of Žiča was indeed the greatest figure in our Church since the time of St Sava. Your words will be heard by all the Serbs, those in Yugoslavia[2] as well as those in exile. They there and we here all owe you a debt of gratitude, and your words will echo in our hearts.[3]

Bishop Bell also received a letter from K. St. Pavlović, chairman of the Council of St. Sava's Church, also dated September 24th:[4]

---

1. The Revd Miloje Nikolić was Protopriest of the Serbian Orthodox Church in London from 1944 to 1988. There is an obituary notice of him by Zaga Gavrilović in *Sobornost*, Vol. 11 (1989), pp. 92-94.

2. It would be interesting to know whether the text of George Bell's sermon was available in Yugoslavia in 1956.

3. *Bell Papers*, Vol. 79, f. 166.

4. *Ibid.*, f. 167.

My Lord Bishop,

I am still under the deepest impression of the most wonderful words you have used last Sunday in paying such a whole-hearted tribute to one we Serbs consider to be one of the greatest among us. His passing was a great blow to all the Serbs, those in Yugoslavia who are not free to express their sorrow, and those in exile who have lost their spiritual leader.

We are all inclined to exaggerate the deeds of our own people, and to minimise those of foreigners. In the case of the late Bishop of Žiča I think that your praise is the best proof that ours was not exaggerated.

It is difficult for me to express what I felt, listening to your words, not only what I personally felt, but also what we all felt, and our feelings go further and deeper than words can say.

May I be allowed, my Lord Bishop, to express to you my most sincere gratitude as well as that of all our Orthodox Community for all you have done and are doing for our cause, and especially for your most touching tribute to our late Bishop ...

The effect of George Bell's memorial sermon is the more remarkable because he was not generally considered to be a very impressive speaker;[5] moreover he was getting old, and even his dynamic energy was beginning to flag.[6] It was the emotional force behind his words that made his sermon so moving; and that in itself was the expression of the deep love and admiration that he felt for Bishop Nikolai, from the time of their first meeting up to the end of Bishop Nikolai's life.

George Bell remained Bishop of Chichester until February, 1958; he retired just after his 75th birthday.[7] He enjoyed only a brief period of retirement - which was, in fact, very active - and

5. See Frank Field, *George Bell: a Uniquely Consistent Life*, p. 58; see also above, p. 56.
6. Jasper, *George Bell*, pp. 383-4; Owen Chadwick, *Michael Ramsey*, p. 97.
7. Jasper, *George Bell*, p. 378.

died on October 3rd, 1958, after a short illness.[8] And so the
friendship passed on to what Bishop Nikolai, in one of his last
letters to George Bell, described as the 'Higher World'.[9]

It was certainly a remarkable friendship, not least on account
of its historical context. There had been contact between the
Church of England and different Orthodox Churches since the
seventeenth century; however for the most part these had been
conducted at an official level, between highly placed Church
leaders, and expressed in formal and elaborate language.[10] It is
only rarely that we catch a glimpse of ordinary individuals and
their everyday activities and relationships.[11] Examples of close
personal friendships within the framework of Inter-Church relations
seem to have been even less frequent; or if they did exist, their
story has not yet been told.

The relationship between George Bell and Nikolai
Velimirović is in fact a good example of what is known as 'soul-
friendship'. This is well-attested in Christian literature from its earliest
times,[12] especially monastic literature. It is an essentially personal
relationship, in which the bond once formed between individuals
can transcend differences of age, nationality and cultural background, and which even seems to be strengthened by periods of
separation; these seem to make meetings more significant and
deeply-experienced when they do occur. In the case of these
two bishops, the seed of their friendship seems to have been
sown during the First World War, when George Bell read
the proofs of Fr. Nikolai's (as he then was) early writings in

---

8. *Ibid.*, pp. 385-6.

9. *Bell Papers*, Vol. 79, f. 144.

10. See, for example, the correspondence quoted in Bell's biography of Archbishop
Randall Davidson, pp. 416-424, 484-5.

11. There is one such example which has been well documented and attractively
presented in Dr Colin Davey's book, *Pioneer for Unity* (British Council of
Churches, 1987).

12. See Kenneth Leech, *Soul Friend* (London, 1961).

English;[13] and it reached its final, powerful expression in the sermon George Bell preached at the memorial service for Bishop Nikolai in September, 1956. An important landmark along the way was their reunion after the Second World War when Bishop Nikolai, then an exile and broken in health, sought out his old friend soon after he arrived in England to take part in the christening of the heir to the exiled King Peter of Yugoslavia. Their subsequent meeting, recorded in detail in George Bell's journal, clearly made a deep impression on both of them,[14] and affected their future relationship, right up to the time of Bishop Nikolai's death, though in these years their circumstances and lifestyle were very different, and their opportunities for meeting became increasingly rare.

Although the friendship between George Bell and Nikolai Velimirović was essentially a personal relationship, the fact that they both were influential Church leaders (whose influence would almost certainly have been stronger but for the events and aftermath of the Second World War) meant that their friendship was also a powerful ecumenical statement. They belonged to different Churches, which had developed differently in the course of many centuries; and each of them was deeply rooted in his own tradition, and completely loyal to it. But the close bond between them showed that there is a spiritual force which transcends these loyalties, though it does not deny them. This was their legacy to future generations.

Such friendships are important in the life of all Churches. In more recent times there has been another well-publicised friendship between two bishops working in Liverpool: the Anglican Bishop David Sheppard and the Roman Catholic Archbishop

---

13. See Appendix I, p. 101.
14. See above, p. 65ff.

Derek Worlock described in their book, *Better Together*.[15] And there are also many people today, not in the public eye, who have come to share the same experience when they meet at conferences or on pilgrimages, or work together on social and humanitarian projects, or simply meet as friends or neighbours. To all these people, the story of the friendship between George Bell and Nikolai Velimirović must surely be a source of inspiration and encouragement.

15. It seems that this friendship is vividly remembered in Liverpool; a recent comment in the *Tablet* (March 13th, 1999) relating to the appointment of a new Anglican bishop of Liverpool, says: 'What everyone wants to know is if the Bishop David Sheppard will be repeated' *(Notebook, p. 368)*.

APPENDIX I

Bishop Nikolai was a prolific writer throughout his life, mainly in his native language; but he also wrote a number of works in English. Most of these were written either while he was living in England during the First World War, or during the later part of his life when he was living in exile in America. His writings in English dating from the time of the First World War, mainly short pamphlets, are of considerable interest, both for the light they throw on his spiritual and intellectual development, and as historical source-material for that period. As they are now rare works (carefully preserved in Lambeth Palace Library), it seems relevant to the present study to list them and give a brief indication of their content. They are here treated in chronological order.

Religion and Nationality in Serbia (1915, pp. 23), translated by Fanny Copeland, with a Prefatory Note by R.W. Seton-Watson, who writes:

No apology is needed for placing this remarkable little pamphlet within reach of the British public, for it deals with a subject which deserves greater attention at the present time, and strikes a highly interesting and sympathetic note.

The main theme of this work (not obvious from the title) is the need for the Roman Catholic and Orthodox Churches to work together for the welfare of the future 'Yugoslav' state, which (as Fr Nikolai points out) 'will contain about 50 dioceses, half of them Catholic, and the other Orthodox'(p. 20). He ends on an optimistic note: 'All we Jugoslavs are sure that there will be harmony and unity between our priesthoods, the two confessions, and the two Churches of the Serbian state' (p. 22). Sadly, this confident expectation was not fulfilled.

This short work is dedicated to the memory of Bishop Joseph Strossmayer, Croat patriot and pioneer champion of Christian unity, on the occasion of the centenary of his birth in 1815.

Serbia's Place in Human History (October, 1915 pp. 26). Published by the Council for the Study of International Relations, and dedicated to R.W. Seton-Watson.

This begins with a short philosophical essay on the theme that small nations have the right to an independent political and cultural existence, and should not be dominated and ruled by larger ones. Then there follows a summary of the main landmarks of Serbian history: the development of the medieval state; the battle of Kosovo and its aftermath; the revolt against Turkish rule at the beginning of the 19th century; and the current struggle against Austria and Germany during the First World War. 'Serbia is now fighting,' he says, 'not only for her own independence, but also for the freedom of all her enslaved brethren, Serbs, Croats and Slovenes under the rule of Austria' (p. 15).

Sermons on Subjects Suggested by the War (London, 1916, pp. 40).

These were the sermons delivered by Fr Nikolai at St Margaret's, Westminster, in March, 1916 (see above, p. 7), under the titles *Slav Orthodoxy* (pp. 1-14); *Slav Revolutionary Catholicism,* (pp. 17-27); and *The Religious Spirit of the Slavs,* (pp. 31-40). It is difficult to summarize their content, as they are so wide-ranging in subject matter and so densely packed with arresting images and challenging assertions. The following extracts give some idea of their quality. In discussing the theme that 'The Christian Church is always on trial', he says that t he Orthodox Churches have 'stood the test very well' in times of persecution and domination by non-Christian rulers. Then he goes on to say:

> *And Anglicanism? It had the worst enemy. That was wealth, comfort, quiet business, lack of big disturbances and of great sufferings. The English Church still succeeded in preventing all the misuses and abuses of life under such circumstances ... Yet English Christianity is neither so dramatic and full of contrasts as Dante's Catholicism, nor so vibrating a lyric as Dostojevsky's Orthodoxy, but rather a quiet smooth epic, like Milton's poetry* (p. 4).

And then at the end of this sermon:

> *For centuries Slav Orthodoxy seemed to the Western world like an immobile tortoise with a multi-coloured shell, and with no great probability of its being inhabited by a living being ... I will try to show you that there was and still is a living being contained therein, with many more movements, dis-satisfactions, convulsions, longings and sufferings than it seems possible should exist* (p. 14).

The Lord's Prayer: a Devout Interpretation (Church of England Men's Society, 1916), with a foreword by the Archbishop of York.

This short work, unlike Fr Nikolai's other writings in English at this time, is a purely devotional work: an extended meditation on the separate sentences of the Lord's Prayer.

Serbia in Light and Darkness (London, Longmans, 1916).
With a preface by the Archbishop of Canterbury.

This is a longer and more complex work than those previously described. The first section consists of sermons and lectures delivered by Fr Nikolai: *England and Serbia*, delivered in the Chapter House of Canterbury Cathedral (pp. 3-23); *Serbia for Cross and Freedom*, delivered at Holy Trinity Church, Strond Green, London (pp. 24-47); *Serbia at Peace*, New Lecture Rooms, Cambridge (pp. 48-73); and *Serbia in Arms*, an address to English soldiers (pp. 74-103). Then there follows a section entitled *Fragments of Serbian National Wisdom* (pp. 107-130), consisting mainly of translated extracts from Serbian epic poetry, taken from an English translation published in 1827: *Serbian Popular Poetry*, by John Bowring. The book includes several illustrations, both photographs (historically interesting in themselves) and reproductions of Serbian nineteenth-century paintings.

In the talk on *Serbia at Peace*, Fr Nikolai gives a moving description of family prayers during his childhood, when the family met at the end of the day's work:

> *We had no chapel in the house. In bad weather we prayed in the house, in fine weather out of doors. My grandfather took a chalice with fire and incense, and sprinkled every one of us. Then he came forward, bowed deeply, and his example was followed by us all. Then began a silent prayer, interrupted only here and there by a sighing or by some whispering voice. We crossed ourselves and prayed, looking to the earth and looking to the stars. The prayer ended again with deep bowing and a loud 'Amen'.*
>
> *When I recall this prayer in my memory, I feel more piety, more humility and more comfort than I ever felt in any of the big cathedrals in either hemisphere where I have had the opportunity of praying* (pp. 71-2).

The above writings were mainly connected with the events of the First World War. Another important work written by Bishop Nikolai shortly after the war was *The Spiritual Rebirth of Europe*, published by the Faith Press in 1920.

APPENDIX II

The situation which Bishop Nikolai referred to in a letter to George Bell as a 'boiling kettle' is a little-known and somewhat complicated aspect of ecclesiastical history.

Shortly after the establishment of the Czechoslovak Republic in 1919, a reformist movement developed in the Catholic Church there. The reformers drew their inspiration from the Cyrillo-Methodian and the Hussite experience of their ancestors, both suppressed and long dormant as a result of the domination of the Jesuits in the Czech Church since the seventeenth century. Their programme included, among other things, the abolition of compulsory celibacy for the priesthood, and the use of the vernacular language in the liturgy.

One of their leaders, Matthias Pavlik, was ordained as an Orthodox bishop, taking the name of Gorazd (one of the disciples of Constantine and Methodius during the Moravian mission of 863). It was he and his followers who entered into negotiations with the Serbian Orthodox Church in 1920. However most of the reformers, who favoured more radical policies, founded a separate dissident body, known as the Czechoslovak National Church.

Later the followers of Bishop Gorazd became the nucleus of a Czech Orthodox Church, which gained autocephalous status in 1951.

Index

Index